The *Zen Writings* Series

ON ZEN PRACTICE

ON ZEN PRACTICE

Edited by Hakuyu Taizan Maezumi
and Bernard Tetsugen Glassman

Zen Writings Series

Zen Center Of Los Angeles

Publications of the Zen Center of Los Angeles

ZCLA Journal: Yasutani Roshi Memorial Issue
                Zen and Science Issue

Zen Writings Series: On Zen Practice *(1976)*
                      On Zen Practice II *(1977)*
                      To Forget the Self: An Illustrated Introduction
                                        To Zen Practice *(1977)*

Frontispiece

Boy and Buffalo, by Sekkyakushi
Muromachi period, 15th century A.D.
Hanging scroll, ink on paper
Asian Art Museum of San Francisco
Avery Brundage Collection

On Zen Practice is the first volume in the *Zen Writings* monographic series which comprises two new titles a year, with occasional supplementary releases. Donation for two volumes a year: $7.00 in the U.S., $9.00 foreign. Single-volume donation: $4.00. For information about subscriptions or distribution, contact Zen Writings, 927 South Normandie Avenue, Los Angeles, California 90006. ISBN: 0-916820-02-5. Library of Congress Card Catalogue Number: 76-9463. Published by Zen Center of Los Angeles, Inc., 927 South Normandie Avenue, Los Angeles, California 90006, a non-profit religious corporation. © 1976 by Zen Center of Los Angeles, Inc. All rights reserved. Printed in the United States of America. Second edition ©1976

CONTENTS

To The Reader:

Among the many books in English on Zen Buddhism, few are entirely based upon actual practice. Most deal with a variety of theoretical and cultural topics, while some set forth general principles of practice. This book and its companion volume, *On Zen Practice II*, are a little different. They are a composite portrait of practice as conducted at the Zen Center of Los Angeles (ZCLA). Because Maezumi Roshi represents three distinct teaching traditions within Zen, there is a certain richness and diversity of approach. We have sought in these books, to preserve something of the characteristic style and feel of ZCLA training. They reflect a living community, with personality and idiosyncracies left intact.

American Zen is taking root and growing strong; at times it is ungainly and raw, but it is also vigorous and unique in its own right. We offer these books to the reader hoping to encourage him in his practice, and to afford the public a clearer, more accurate picture of what Zen practice is all about.

John Daishin Buksbazen
Publishing Editor

Riverside Village on a Late Autumn Day
Ma Yuen
Late 12th-Early 13th C. Sung
Courtesy Museum of Fine Arts, Boston

Ascending to the high seat, [Dōgen Zenji] said:

"Zen Master Hōgen studied with Keishin Zenji. Once Keishin Zenji asked him, 'Joza, where do you go?'

"Hōgen said, 'I am making pilgrimage aimlessly.'

"Keishin said, 'What is the matter of your pilgrimage?'

"Hōgen said, 'I don't know.'

"Keishin said, 'Not knowing is the most intimate.'

"Hōgen suddenly attained great enlightenment."

Master [Dōgen] said: "If I, Kosho[1], were there, I would have said to Priest Jizo[2], 'Not knowing is the most intimate. Knowing is also the most intimate. Let's leave intimacy for the most intimate. Then tell me: with what are you the most intimate?'"

—Dōgen Zenji, *Ehei koroku*
(Translated by Taizan Maezumi Roshi)

---

1. Kosho is another name for Dōgen Zenji.
2. Priest Jizo refers to Keishin Zenji who lived in Jizo-In Temple.

1

WHY PRACTICE?

Taizan Maezumi Roshi

"This Dharma (the subtle Dharma which has been transmitted by all Buddha-Tathagatas) is abundantly inherent in each individual; yet without practice it will not be manifested, and without enlightenment it will not be perceived."

•

". . . Since it is the practice of enlightenment, that practice has no beginning and since it is enlightenment within the practice, that realization has no end."

Dōgen Zenji: *Shōbōgenzō, Bendōwa*

People practice Zen for many reasons. For some, it is a means to establish better physical and emotional health. For others, it leads into the realization of their own (non-Buddhist) religion or philosophy. And for some Zen practice is the living experience of what Shakyamuni taught.

Now it is not unusual for people to complain that "religion" or "philosophy" are not relevant to their lives. They are looking for more than words or concepts alone. And I tend to agree with them that words and concepts by themselves are indeed inadequate to help us live our lives with the greatest awareness and growth of which we are capable.

Practice is like regular exercise, which builds strength, gracefulness, and self-confidence, to meet the situations we all face every day. And it is like a laboratory, in which we can continuously test our understanding to see if it is adequate or not. If we never test our beliefs, we cannot find out their truth or falseness.

3

When Shakyamuni Buddha first realized his true nature (and, in so doing, realized the true nature of all beings) he said that from the first, all beings are intrinsically perfect, absolute, sharing the virtues and wisdom of the Buddha. But, he said, we remain unaware of this simply because our understanding is topsy-turvy. Then he spent the remainder of his life enlarging upon this statement, and pointing out how we can all realize this fact through practice.

It is as though we had an uncut diamond. We could not really say that it was worthless, or say it was something other than a diamond. But unless skillfully cut and meticulously polished, its diamond-nature might not be visible. The beautiful color and clarity which make it so highly prized would remain in the realm of potential.

Of course, we might sincerely *believe* it to be a diamond. We might even tell others, "This is a diamond and worth a lot." Yet it would seem peculiar to say, "I don't need to cut and polish this diamond. I know that it is a diamond, and that's good enough for me." Rather, we must cut that diamond and polish its many facets carefully in order that its lovely nature might be shared and enjoyed by all who see it. So it is with our practice. We don't wish to make diamonds out of mud—we wish to properly appreciate what is already inherent.

But it must be done physically. Our whole practice rests upon a physical base, just as our lives begin physically. First we learn to bring our bodies into harmony—we learn to sit physically Once that happens, our breathing naturally settles into a harmonious cycle—we stop panting and gasping, and start to breathe easily, smoothly, and naturally. And as body and breath settle down and no longer create disturbances for us, we find that the mind itself is given the opportunity to settle into its own smooth and natural functioning. The racket and babble of our noisy minds give way to the clarity and naturalness of our true selves. In this way we come to know who we really are, and what our life and death really is.

Finally, once we begin to establish this direct physical harmony between body, breath, and mental activity, we have a chance to extend such benefits to one another. We can learn to live together in the best way, leading to the realization of everyone's true nature on not only an individual but also a group level as well.

This kind of group practice, such as at a Zen center, can be of real benefit to a world such as ours. Perhaps it is not so irrelevant to a world in which harmony is scarcer even than diamonds, and in which the realization of Truth is widely regarded as an impossible dream.

In fact, we can say that the Three Treasures of Buddhism—Buddha, Dharma, and Sangha—are altogether nothing more or less than practice. The Buddha is the one who realizes. The Dharma is what is realized. And the Sangha is the harmony of practice, both communal and individual, in accord with the Buddha-way. In this way, all relationships teach us, even as we appreciate and polish each other, endlessly.

CHAPTER 1

WHAT IS PRACTICE?
Dharma Dialogue (Shosan)

Shōsan or Dharma Dialogue, is a centuries-old method of
Zen training. Recently introduced into the practice of
American Zen students, *shōsan* is a free-wheeling give and
take between practicing Zen monks, nuns, and laypersons.
Students come up in turn and have dialogue with the
shōsanshi, or leader, usually the Zen master or a senior
monk of the group.

This *shōsan* occurred in June 1975, during the Summer
Training Period at Zen Center of Los Angeles. *Shōsanshi*
was Bernard Tetsugen Glassman. Dharma names of the
participants are used whenever possible.

Tetsugen's Opening Remarks: Last March, as a theme for *shōsan*, I
talked about *buji* Zen and practice. At that time very few people came
up with questions or statements, so I'd like to cover this subject again,
since it's such an important theme during ango. Please feel free, or
please feel compelled, to come up.

Yasutani Roshi was severely critical of *buji* Zen. *Buji* Zen means
'no matter Zen.' In our study we view Zen from both intrinsic and
experiential perspectives. From the intrinsic point of view, everything
as it is is perfect. The sutras say the Way *is* everything, nothing is excluded. All sentient beings *are* Buddha. Dōgen Zenji said, "Enlightenment is
delusion. Delusion is enlightenment." Hearing these statements or taking
these statements as they are, it becomes natural that *buji* Zen develops.
People take these statements and say, "Everything I do, that's the Way.
Everybody, including myself, is Buddha. So who needs a zendo? Whatever I feel is the appropriate thing—that's the Perfect Way. As long as I
lead my life the way I feel is best, that's the Buddha Way."

In Japan we see many scholars teaching in Buddhist Universities, practicing *buji* Zen, lecturing on *buji* Zen. In this country, naturally, *buji* Zen is developing. But just as naturally, critics of *buji* Zen are developing. In Japan Yasutani Roshi attacked *buji* Zen very strongly.

Dōgen Zenji, reading the statements, "All Sentient Beings are the Buddha. Everything as is is the Way," asked (and I'm not sure how old he was, maybe ten years old), "If that's so, why did all the Patriarchs, all the masters, practice so hard? Why do we read stories about ten, twenty, thirty, forty years of training before one becomes a teacher?" That question became a burning flame, and he went from priest to priest trying to find the answer. Dōgen practiced koan study, and he completed koan study; then he practiced shikan-taza. Finally, he resolved the question. That's experiential Zen.

If we stick only to the intrinsic perspective, that's no good—that's *buji* Zen. You can develop a vast vocabulary of all the appropriate words and statements, and understand lectures, but definitely, something will come up in life and you'll be shaken. Without each one of us experiencing those statements personally, so that they're our statements, they're worthless—just a good parlor game where you talk about Zen but never live it.

As a means of helping us to experience the truth, teachers and Patriarchs taught zazen as the primary, most important, key element. Along with zazen, other things developed: zendo, sesshin, ango, *shōsan*, koan study, dokusan. We hear that my practice is the practice of working, eating and sleeping. In koan study we deal with koans like this, and it's true. But always, if those statements are just being made from an intrinsic standpoint, they're no good.

Our focus here is zazen. Definitely Zen will develop in this country, and definitely we will be the ones who will make Zen develop in this country. And the only way is to realize this Buddha Way and to actualize it. Dōgen Zenji defined the prosperity of a monastery, or in our case of the Zen Center, by saying if a monastery has five hundred, a thousand monks, and if their practice is weak, that monastery is not progressing. If a monastery has two, three, five, ten monks and the practice is strong, that monastery is progressing, prospering. Tell me, what is practice? Please come up.

Genpo: *Shōsanshi*! You ask, "What is practice?" Practice is eating, sleeping, sitting in the zendo, going to dokusan, gaining, throwing it out.

Tetsugen: Dōgen Zenji said, "Delusion is enlightenment. Enlightenment is delusion." You just listed all the items of delusion. What is enlightenment?

Genpo: Delusion.

Tetsugen: It's not good enough.

Genpo: So I'll throw it out.

Tetsugen: Then you'll have it.

Genpo: Thank you for your answer.

●

Julie: Tetsugen, I have two questions. The first is, when I first came here I was really . . . I was a very desperate woman, and I really wanted to be enlightened. I couldn't live without it. And now it's important to practice, but I don't think about enlightenment. Is that wrong?

Tetsugen: We talk about major elements in our practice: one being faith, one being desire. Each of us are somewhere in this spectrum. There are some people with strong faith and they practice. If they keep practicing definitely they'll open their eyes. Some people have strong desire, push and drive; they have to get enlightened. If they continue to push, definitely it will happen. Some people are in between, and if they practice, definitely it will happen.

Julie: My second question is a question that I've been wanting to
            ask you for a long time. Has having kensho experience made
            any difference in your life?

Tetsugen: Ask my wife. (laughter)

Julie: She would know. Thank you.

•

Sotetsu: *Shōsanshi*, practice is seeing. Is there anything else?

Tetsugen: Always, there are two things, then one above that. Practice is
            seeing. Every morning, we chant, "Form is emptiness. Empti-
            ness is form." We have to see both sides, then go above both.
            What's the other side of "Practice is seeing?"

Sotetsu: Not seeing.

Tetsugen: No. See the other side.

•

Szabolcs: *Shōsanshi*, you ask, "What is practice?" What is not practice?

Tetsugen: That's *buji* Zen.

Szabolcs: But, what is not practice?

Tetsugen: Not-practice is practicing without seeing, and that's *buji* Zen.

Szabolcs: As the head in the zendo, how do you stop not-practice?

Tetsugen: As *tantō* in the zendo, I don't stop not-practice; you have to
            stop it. Each one of us has to stop it. But don't try to stop
            somebody else.

Szabolcs: Thank you.

•

Ryoshin: *Shōsanshi*, I, too, have that burning question of it's all okay but I'm not all okay—Why? And I've become lots of problems for myself and for other people, trying to make other people stop not-practicing, like you just said . . . trying to run the universe.

You are a person one could call a technocrat. In today's society we have certain kinds of scientifically-oriented managers. I know for a number of years you worked in the business world in that function. I, too, did some things like that. So in extending myself in practice from just sitting motionless on a cushion into more and more complex situations, I have a lot of questions, a lot of difficulties in dealing with them. Specifically, my question to you is: In Buddhism we talk about three principle bodhisattvas—wisdom, love and compassion. These three virtues. Would you please express the interrelationship of wisdom, love, and compassion functioning in the business world. (Laughter.) It's a big question, I know, really big.

Tetsugen: No, it's a small question.

Ryoshin: I know we keep saying that. It is small, but it's not easy.

Tetsugen: It's the same answer whether it's the business world, whether it's the whatever world. The world's the world.

Wisdom. We've got Manjusri on the altar. That's the wisdom we talk about. That wisdom is the functioning of samadhi, the natural functioning of samadhi. Love is the natural functioning of wisdom. This wisdom is seeing that we're one. No divisions. In that case, love is right there. If your hand is on fire, you pull it out; if your back itches, you scratch it. Normally, we talk about love always in a dualistic sense, loving someone else. We don't think about loving our hand, but that's the love of Samantabhadra Bodhisattva. And the direct functioning of love is compassion, Kannon Bodhisattva. So they're all there at the same time . . . or none of them are there. And that's why we have to practice. If we try to *make* any one there, it's impossible. You're defiling Manjusri Bodhisattva.

Ryoshin: That's right.

Tetsugen: But, definitely, practice will show that all of them are nothing but us and they'll be all there. That's why we appreciate each one of them each day we appreciate ourselves. It just may not look that way right now.

Ryoshin: That's the point. In the zendo, things are made easier for us so that we have to deal with less things. Specifically, there are certain procedures that have been set up by masters, by seniors. This morning at the *gakki* service, five people had to function together to get the *sambō* to the altar in a prescribed manner. Those five people have been practicing that thing for a while, and there were procedures set up in which they could study the actions and then put themselves into it as best they could. Outside of this room in our functioning there are other prescribed procedures. Take gardening: certain ways you do things make trees grow; do something else, trees don't grow. In organizational techniques, where you have many people to deal with, there are volumes and volumes of books written on the subject and many schools where people study them. Still we make problems because we aren't really clear. So that's why I asked you; perhaps you could show me an expression—not tell me how it will be when I'm all clear, how it really is anyway—but show experientially how this oneness comes up appropriately.

Tetsugen: In Zen we talk about pecking and chicking. Are those the right words?

Ryoshin: Pardon?

Tetsugen: Pecking and chicking.

Ryoshin: Pecking and chicking? Checking?

Tetsugen: No.

Ryoshin: Checking, pecking, chicking.

Tetsugen: Peck, peck! Chick, chick!
When a chicken is about to hatch from inside of an egg, it starts with this little beak going peck, peck against the egg. The mother hears it and helps crack the shell from the outside —chick, chick. You do it too soon, the chicken dies. You do it too late, it suffocates. Teachers and Patriarchs developed this training technique, devised procedures. This is a training ground. The zendo office is a proving ground. Both are essential. You don't make the whole world the zendo; you don't make the whole world the office. There are offices and there are zendos, and there are purposes for both. Our key purpose is to get to that place where we're peck, peck, pecking.

Ryoshin: That's right.

Tetsugen: That's all I can say to you.

Ryoshin: I'll work on that. Thank you for your answer.

●

Sojun: *Shōsanshi*, Ryoshin was asking how you see the bodhisattvas functioning in the world. When he said that, I thought of Watergate being cleaned up and Ralph Nader attacking General Motors. What do you say?

Tetsugen: That's half—and you should see Watergate; you should see General Motors. And that's the other half.

Sojun: Are you satisfied?

Tetsugen: I hope I'm never satisfied.

●

Joan: As a musician, I've had trouble with the use of the word prac-
           tice because for us, it means perhaps something a little
           different, as opposed to performance. Is there a difference?

Tetsugen: Only in the way we look at it. As a musician, it seems like it
           would be nice if every practice were the performance.

Joan: What if it isn't?

Tetsugen: Then it's dualism, it's practice and performance, it's being in
           the zendo and being outside the zendo. It should be the same
           thing.

Joan: In here too?

Tetsugen: Everywhere. As I mentioned earlier, the only distinction
           between practice and non-practice is in seeing. If we form a
           split, a separation between us and what we're doing, then we
           can't say that practice is performance. Then you're using
           practice in the way you're using it in the musical sense, not
           the way we're using it here. When I say practice, there's no
           split, no division. And I believe that's what you call perform-
           ance.

Joan: What about between study and application?

Tetsugen: Same thing. You've heard the famous saying: When you eat,
           eat; when you sleep, sleep; the same thing.

Joan: What's the same thing?

Tetsugen: What's the same thing? Please find out what's the same thing.

•

Chiko: *Shōsanshi*, my life goes up and down—sometimes, my head's really clear and everything's groovy and fine and I don't feel like *buji* Zen exists at all. Then, other times, I have absolutely no touch with myself or anything, and I'm just way out there somewhere. I don't have much control in my practice. I may be way out somewhere else, and then suddenly, unexpectedly everything is clear; and I don't know how to consciously get in touch. I can be sitting and suddenly, it happens, I'm in touch. Can you say something to me about this?

Tetsugen: I don't personally feel that by reasoning and analysis you can resolve that problem.

Chiko: But how does it work? I don't know how it works.

Tetsugen: If you ask me I would say that certainly there are different levels of yourself with which to be in touch. I don't think that the deeper levels can be reached by rational, analytical means.

Chiko: Yeah.

Tetsugen: I mean of getting to the point where you're really stable, centered. Certainly, lots of things can be done on a conscious level, the way of working to straighten things up. But I think always, we're shaken up. The way to really solve that, to satisfy that type of stability, I personally feel, is through zazen. I think one of our problems is impatience. One of the names of Shakyamuni Buddha was "He-who-is-able-to-be-patient." We read about studying for ten, twenty, forty years, and it seems like eternity. We want six-week treatments.

Chiko: Yeah, but it gets real hard to live in hell all the time.

Tetsugen: It's real hard to live anywhere. (Laughter.)

Chiko: It's nice when things are groovy, though.

Tetsugen: Yeah, but if you're always living in the heavens, then you always have to fall.

Chiko: I'm not talking about heavens, I'm talking about just when . . . well, you know what I mean.

Tetsugen: Well, I associate "groovy" with heavens. (Laughter.)

Chiko: I associate "groovy" with being able to get through the day and everything. (Laughter.) This is getting crazy.

Tetsugen: Yeah. I'm really serious, though, about Patience Paramita . . .

Chiko: Yeah.

Tetsugen: . . . and about people expecting to come sit on the zafu and have the whole world straightened out in a week, six months, a year, five years. We all start from different places, different potentials. If you read about the great Zen masters, none of them practiced for just six months. If we would compare ourselves to them, and look at the number of years they practiced before they felt okay, or satisfied, then—please just practice.

Chiko: You're pretty stable; how do you do it?

Tetsugen: I practice.

Chiko: Um, I can see that.

Tetsugen: And you may not believe it, but I'm very patient.

Chiko: Yeah, okay. Thank you for your answer.

•

Ryokaku: *Shōsanshi*, last night in watching fireworks, for one moment, I was just watching fireworks; I was not doing anything else. How do I keep that throughout the rest of my life?

Tetsugen: You don't.

Ryokaku: By not doing it, am I practicing?

Tetsugen: If we try to do anything in particular, then it's like decorating the cage that we're in. Maybe enlarging the cage we're in, maybe changing its shape. What we want to do is break it apart, destroy that cage. Many times, I hear people saying, "How do I get to such and such a place? How do I become such and such?" In Zen practice we destroy that cage to where there's nothing to hold onto or stand on. And that's what our practice is about. Practice with the Roshi, and you'll see what that means.

Ryokaku: Thank you for your answer.

•

Ann: Is practice flowing with each minute, or is practice being aware of each minute?

Tetsugen: Neither, it's being.

Ann: Thank you for your answer.

•

Shishin: You said everything is perfect as is. Why do we have to make such a great effort?

Tetsugen: You're not Dōgen Zenji.

Shishin: I had that question before I heard that Dōgen Zenji had it. (Laughter.)

Tetsugen: You're 700 years too late. But seriously, if you have that question, then you've got to answer it. Dōgen Zenji answered it himself. He asked that question of many, many teachers. They couldn't answer it. But having the question, really having the question—I don't mean just parroting someone's words—really having the question is one half of the practice. And the other half is resolving it.

Shishin: As a scientist, my effort is manifest in certain ways. Like Chiko, sometimes I feel as if I'm sitting very well and deeper into my practice than other times, and I have tried to pursue it by checking my disposition each time I sit—my body, my tongue, how my eyes are, my breathing—and it doesn't seem to have anything to do with whether my sitting is good or not. Is there any rationality in this practice? (Laughter.)

Tetsugen: No.

●

Jisho: You were talking to Ryokaku about breaking out of the cage instead of decorating it. It all . . .

Tetsugen: Ah, no.

Jisho: Oh.

Tetsugen: If you break out of it, it's still there.

Jisho: Oh, if we get rid of it. The thing I fear is that if we do that, we will put an end to physical life.

Tetsugen: No.

Jisho: So, it's how to do that without putting an end to physical life?

Tetsugen: Putting an end to physical life won't do that.

Jisho: Oh, okay, you've deepened my problem. (Laughter.)

●

Jocelyn: I don't feel I'm practicing *buji* Zen, but I'm not practicing well. Even when I'm sitting, I don't feel I'm practicing; and my faith in enlightenment is sort of halfhearted. The Buddha said that's the way it is, so I just take his word for it. I'd like to know how I could make this a stronger type of faith and practice.

Tetsugen: I feel that it will either happen or it won't. And practicing here, doing zazen, sitting, is continuing along the road that we're practicing with the Roshi. You'll get to a point where those things will deepen, or they won't and you'll leave. There's nothing wrong either way. I'd like the former one, but that's because I'm attached.

Jocelyn: (Laughs.)

Tetsugen: But it has· to naturally, spontaneously come up from inside of you. It might be that what comes is a very strong faith which will further strengthen your practice. Or it might develop that what comes up is a very strong determination, a resolution to answer some kind of burning flame. If that happens, that will strengthen your practice. And it might happen that you'll just get tired and say, "What's this all about?" and leave.

Jocelyn: Thank you for your answer.

●

Richard: *Shōsanshi*, you spoke of tearing down cages. My experience in
           practice is that one cage goes down and another goes up—the
           next one, hopefully, being larger and giving us more room.
           But this appears as a successive process. The question to you
           is how to deal with the moment when the walls go down be-
           fore any landmarks appear?

Tetsugen: That very moment is the manifestation of Manjusri Bodhi-
           sattva, wisdom. You don't deal with it. The functioning of
           that very moment is Samantabhadra Bodhisattva, love, com-
           passion, Kannon Bodhisattva. You don't deal with it. As soon
           as you deal with it, you've built your bigger cage, or your
           smaller one. What happens in that moment, instead of you
           dealing with it, is *It* deals. Let me add one thing, for Susan's
           (Jisho's) sake. In that moment, *It* deals in an extremely alive
           and active manner.

●

Ryoshin: *Shōsanshi*, please . . . allow me to knock my head against that
           cage once more. I heard a Zen master a few years ago say,
           "Zen practice is washing away dirt with dirt." Seems to be
           what's happening. Like for instance, this last month a lot of
           dirt came up right here and a lot of dirt got washed away.
           Roshi says working in the kitchen would be very good for
           your practice, but working in the kitchen can also ruin your
           practice. Who determines, what determines, which person
           goes in what position and how much dirt gets stirred up
           through moving how much other dirt? Does anybody? Or
           does it just happen, and we all have to kick up this dirt and
           then something else comes up? Like, what happens?

Kwannon Bosatsu
Scroll Painting
by Hakuin Zenji
(1686-1789)

Tetsugen: Technically, it's called the karmic law of causation, which
doesn't answer anything. Certainly, it's not arbitrary. You've
got some hidden questions underneath which I think would
be better not to talk about here. But as Roshi has said, you
have to look at the time, the place, the person, and the amount
or degree. They are the four key elements in deciding just
about anything, including assignment of people to various
positions. And if they aren't the right people, if it isn't
the right time, and if the duration isn't right, we still have to
make decisions and do that. You do the best you can. But
when we say that the way as it is is perfect, we don't mean
perfect in the sense of everything's just great and dandy. It's
complete. It's what it is. And if there's a lot of frustration,
that's what it is. And if it's a lot of dirt, that's what it is.
If we try to make all that dirt look like what we want it to,
or we try to eliminate all the frustration, or think we can,
we're in for a lot of frustration.

Ryoshin: When we take vows, have jukai and tokudo, we vow not to
get angry. Roshi talked about anger last year. And he said
anger is being separated from ourselves, not being one. And
to repent for that anger is to continuously repent, continuously practice. And when we become a position and continuously violate these precepts blatantly, out of control—like
Chiko said, out of control—is it too much for one's capacity?
Or do we all just go on to the next moment and say that was
necessary?

Tetsugen: Let me relate this to our own body. Many people here have
had jukai, taking the precepts. As Roshi has mentioned, precepts is not such a great word. In Japanese, they say *kai*-*kai*
is a translation of the Sanskrit word, *sila*. I prefer the word
aspect to precept. But that's not quite right, he says. Essentially, though, the *kai* that we take are aspects of ourselves.
And the only way to really maintain the *kai* is fully to become
one with everything.

Ryoshin: Yes.

Tetsugen: If we look at our body as an example of something else we are one with, if something happens in our body, a boil appears, we get a cut, we don't get angry at that boil. That same kind of emotion—if we get a cut, a cut appears and it's a deep one, we rush to do something to take care of it—that same emotion, whatever's going on inside, can be there. That's not anger, that's determination. We're going to get it taken care of. We're going to do the right thing.

Ryoshin: That's right.

Tetsugen: When we use that word anger, by definition we've separated ourselves from what we're getting angry at. It doesn't mean that the same emotion doesn't occur. It's just that being one, instead of anger, it's determination, and it's action.

Ryoshin: Yeah. Thanks. Thank you for your answer.

●

Genki: *Shōsanshi*, I practiced for a long time from the point of wanting to get somewhere—states of consciousness, the oneness with the environment. As long as I did that, I got certain things, but I was continually at war within myself, and really far away from what I actually wanted. Thinking about clarity and wanting clarity, I always had an idea of what that clarity was. It had to be a larger consciousness. It had to be something other than what I was. Even to say I was angry, that wasn't really clarity. Clarity was experiencing a shoulder hunched, teeth gritted, certain stream of thoughts. And the more I sank deeper and deeper into whatever it was I really was—clarity was there. Not even clarity, there was no question, there was no room for me to wonder what I was or what was happening. Do you have anything to say?

Tetsugen: I have nothing to say.

Genki: Thank you.

•

Kando: *Shōsanshi*, there's been a lot of talk about dust. I feel much
          that way, too. Every time I move, I raise a cloud of dust.
          What's to be done about it?

Tetsugen: I hate to repeat myself, but practice.

Kando: Then what I'm doing to try not to raise dust is not-practice.
          How do we find practice?

Tetsugen: That's where we started. I asked that question. When the
          Sixth Patriarch received inka from the Fifth Patriarch, the
          dialogue that went on was very similar. The Sixth Patriarch
          came to the Fifth Patriarch's monastery as a layperson. It was
          a big monastery, maybe 800 monks. And he was assigned the
          job of refining rice. His job was transforming the brown rice
          to white rice. And after nine months of working in the rice
          refinery—you remember those famous poems, they deal direct-
          ly with dust. Priest Jinshu's verse went:

                   Our body is the Bodhi tree,
                   And our mind a mirror bright.
                   Carefully we wipe them hour by hour,
                   And let no dust alight.

          And the Sixth Patriarch responded to that poem:

                   There is no Bodhi-tree,
                   Nor the stand of a mirror bright.
                   Since all is void,
                   Where can the dust alight?

          After the Fifth Patriarch realized the time was ripe for Eno to
          become the Sixth Patriarch, he went to his hut. He hadn't talked

to him now for nine months. He had known at that first visit
that Eno was the man succeeding his Dharma. So, he visited
him that night, and he asked him, "Has the rice become
white?" Is the dust gone? Now, in those nine months, he
hadn't shown him how to make brown rice into white rice.
But Master Eno said, "Yes, the rice is white, but it hasn't
been sifted yet." You need that kind of confidence, to say
the dust is gone.

Kando: I appreciate your answer very much.

●

Concluding Remarks

Tetsugen: As many of you might have noticed, the Zen Center is steadily
growing, and a community is developing. The JOURNAL is
growing; we're getting ready to start publishing books. Members are moving onto the block, buying houses. More people
are working on the staff. And there are more monks. But I'd
like to emphasize that the key element with the Zen Center
is zazen . . . breaking those walls apart into sunyata. Everything else that happens is very important, but the reason we
call this a Zen Center is because the focus, the pivotal point
of all those activities, is our zazen. Please continue to practice
together, with all of us. Thank you.

CHAPTER 2

THE PRACTICE OF EFFORT (VIRYA PARAMITA)
Taizan Maezumi Roshi

This is the fourth in a series of discourses on the Six Paramitas given by Maezumi Roshi. The Six Paramitas are the
teachings of the Buddha. In order, they are listed as Dana
(Giving), Sila (Precepts), Kshanti (Patience), Virya (Effort),
Samadhi (Concentration), and Prajna (Wisdom) Paramitas.
All six are mentioned in the six-hundred volume *Prajna
Paramita Sutra,* of which the well-known Heart Sutra is a
shorter form. The word paramita translates as "reached the
other shore." In actual fact, each paramita contains all the
rest and their practice is the means by which we realize
that other shore right here.

The Effort Paramita, that is the theme for today's talk. Needless to
say, whatever it is we do, be it work or business or studies or anything,
not much can be accomplished without effort. We find this right effort
in practically all of Buddha's major teachings. We even have a common
proverb: "Where there is a will, there is a way."
In the Eight Awarenesses of the Buddha, as the explanation of right
effort, he says this: If you really try, there is nothing which you cannot
accomplish. And he makes an analogy: When you try to start a fire, if
you stop before the wood starts to burn, you will never have combus-
tion. I think in the time of the Buddha fire was made by rubbing sticks

together. There might have been another way to make fire, but maybe rubbing sticks was the most commonly used way to make fire. Also, if water runs or drips continuously, even if only a small amount, eventually it will erode rock. So Buddha warns us to be diligent and to endeavor constantly. For us the point becomes constant, diligent endeavor. But toward what? And how? He tells us something like this: Just continue trying to increase the good that we have done in the past, and also try to do good in the future. In other words, increase the actions or deeds necessary to increase goodness.

The same is true for undesirable things or evil actions. If we have done them in the past, we should try to eliminate them and also try not to let them happen again. Then according to where we are and what kind of work or study we are involved in, we should try to act accordingly. So we can do all sorts of good things, and at the same time we can eliminate all kinds of undesirable things.

This brings to mind another big question.

What is good and what is bad? Right or wrong seem very similar. So, according to the object with which we deal, it differs. And even dealing with the same object, again it differs. I've talked about this before several times. As the elements involved in making a judgment (i.e. time, place and person) change, the values change. Harada Roshi adds amount to these three elements. So, the time, the place, the person involved, and how far or how much—that makes the value judgment different. Then what would be appropriate, adequate, or suitable under such particular circumstances? It's really hard to judge. If ten people get together, there may be ten different opinions. But still we can think according to our experiences and understand the appropriateness of a given situation. An example would be capital punishment. It's exactly related to these fundamental rules, or principles. Some people approve of it according to where they are, according to the time, place, and also the amount—how much punishment is appropriate. But to punish as such is an awful phrase. So some people think capital punishment is too harsh. The amount, see? And regarding the place or time, now it's almost the end of the twentieth century. Capital punishment might have been okay one hundred years ago, or it might not have been okay then. Some people might admit it was happening, others might deny it. According to our conditioning, we carefully think about what it is to be good and what it is to be bad. Then we try to do our best.

These Six Paramitas are set up for monks and nuns, and also for laymen. These principles could be applied generally: in politics, economics, philosophy, psychology or medicine. In the case of terminally ill patients, doctors are faced with the question of whether to help them live longer or let them die sooner. It is hard to judge or evaluate what is right, what is wrong, what is good, what is bad. I leave this part up to you.

Now let us focus upon our own practice. Gathering here together, what is the best thing for us to practice? It is to realize *Anuttara Samyak Sambodhi*, the Supreme Enlightenment. How much can we accomplish is secondary, but it is obvious that it is most important to be oriented in that way. So in order to realize the Supreme Way or Supreme Wisdom, as we are trying to do, we practice. Dōgen Zenji says: "To raise the bodhi mind, before one attains enlightenment oneself, make one's intention to save other people first." Try to accomplish the vow.

Some people say that if we don't become enlightened, we can't help other people. That is not necessarily true. It is, in one sense, so; but if we say so, when can we accomplish it? If we wait until we attain perfect enlightenment, when will it be? It may well never happen. So the way we endeavor is wherever we are, wherever we stand, just have the vows—the Four Great Vows; it's more than enough. Renew these vows and do our best. And doing our best itself is encouraging to other people, helping other people to realize *Anuttara Samyak Sambodhi* together.

We are appreciating Six Paramitas now. Another rather fundamental principle or teaching of the Buddha is called *Shi shō bo*, four things, or four issues, that we should practice as bodhisattvas. The first of the four is giving. The second, loving words. Isn't it nice? In order to say a nice, encouraging, or kind word, we don't need anything. It becomes wonderful giving too. In fact, it's more than giving. The third one is do good things for others, benefit other people. Dōgen Zenji also talks about it, and what he says I really think is true. He says that foolish people might think that if you put other people first, you don't get any benefit; that is not true at all. It benefits both parties. Everyone benefits.

The fourth one is perhaps the hardest to do. It's called the Sameness. Do nothing to others that you would not wish for yourself. I think Christ says the same thing in a reverse way: Do unto others as you would have them do unto you. And Dōgen Zenji says have a heart like the ocean, which holds everything and never complains. It swallows everything—muddy water, clean water, even dead things.

Regarding our practice, so much can be said, such as what is *Anuttara Samyak Sambodhi*? Prajna Paramita, the last of the six paramitas, will help us see this *Anuttara Samyak Sambodhi*, the Supreme Way, Supreme Enlightenment. Prajna itself is wisdom. Combined with the word Paramita, it becomes Supreme Wisdom, wisdom by which we see the Supreme Way; and also we practice the Supreme Way, or more precisely, we realize that everything else is nothing but the Supreme Way. At any rate, let us be diligent.

I notice that when you stand up for kinhin, some of you can't stand up straight and some can't stand at all because your legs are numb. I know it's painful. I have been sitting a little longer than you; my legs are getting used to it, but I recall when I first started sitting. I had an awful, awful time. My left knee was up from the cushion about four or five inches. No matter how I tried, it wouldn't go down! For the nearly two years that I was at Kōryū Roshi's place, nobody told me anything about how to sit. They don't have beginner's instruction such as we have. But this pain is an interesting thing. I notice many of you come to dokusan and talk about pain. "I have so much pain, what can I do about it?" I can't help that. But sometimes people say that having pain helps them concentrate better. I don't know whether that's really true or not, but when you fight pain, sometimes it increases. Then when it gets to a certain point, it disappears. Perhaps you might have been experiencing that, too. You don't have any pain and then try to stand up and find your legs are asleep, utterly numb. Your psychological condition influences your body a great deal, too. So for those who have pain while sitting, I have no definite suggestion about what to do. It would be good to deal with it, not fight it, but try to take care of it nicely. As a matter of fact, many people have attained enlightenment through pain. You may be surprised if I say so, but in a way, Master Rinzai himself did. He was beaten up badly by Master Ōbaku. Then he went to Master

Daigu and he attained enlightenment there. But the direct cause was definitely the sixty blows given bim by Ōbaku.

Also Gensha, whom Dōgen Zenji liked very much, was a fisherman until he was about thirty or thirty-one, then he became a monk. In two years of study he attained enlightenment through pain. He went to Seppō's monastery and stayed only two years. Then he decided to leave the monastery. While he was walking on the road, which was very rocky and hard, he bumped into a rock and he injured his toe very badly. He screamed with pain. What he reflected upon was something like this: The Five Skandhas, body and mind, altogether are empty. Where does this pain come from? *Where does this pain come from?* Under that question, he attained very clear enlightenment. Then without going any place, he returned to Seppō's monastery again. Seppō, seeing Gensha, asked, "What are you doing here? You were supposed to have left. Where were you fooling around?" Then Gensha said to him the famous words: "Bodhidharma never came to China; the Second Patriarch has never left India. Needless to say, Bodhidharma and all other patriarchs are right here with me." I can imagine how happy Seppō would have been. So, if you have pain, use it, and become awakened.

This is Effort Paramita.

CHAPTER 3

WHAT IS SESSHIN?
Taizan Maezumi Roshi

Good morning, everybody.

I see a few new faces. I hope your sitting is comfortable, because when you listen to a talk such as this, I wish you to have the proper disposition of the body, as when you do zazen.

Sesshin consists of from three to seven days of zazen and other activities, while staying here in the zendo. Our yearly schedule now includes at least one such sesshin each month. With this in mind, it would be a good idea to give some thought to what, in general, sesshin means: what is the purpose of having sesshin, and what good it does us in our everyday life. I should like to talk briefly about these things this morning.

Sesshin—if we understand the original implications of the word 'sesshin', we will have a fairly good idea of what it means. It consists of two Chinese ideograms, *setsu* and *shin*. *Shin* is the 'mind', and *setsu* literally means 'to join or to fix together'. To fix the mind together. It really means 'to touch', 'to connect'. And also it means 'to receive', 'to transmit', and 'to continue'. *Setsu* and *shin.* That is, to join or connect the mind, or to receive, transmit, or maintain the mind. That is what sesshin means.

Then our question is: "What is the mind?" This is one of the most ambiguous terms we use. The mind: we can talk about it with common sense, we can talk about it with philosophical concepts, or from a metaphysical standpoint, or using psychological terms, but what is it really?

We talk about my mind, your mind, the Universal Mind, the Cosmic Mind, or capital "M" Mind. To join the Mind or to connect the Mind or to transmit or to receive the Mind, or to maintain the Mind. Now you can guess what sesshin means.

It is to really become one with the Mind.

There is a beautiful passage by Dōgen Zenji about the Mind. He said: "The Mind is the mountains, river, trees, and grass, and the Mind is the sun, the moon, and the stars." That is to say, the whole universe is the Mind itself. And we aren't excluded from that.

We think we have a mind. Okay. Then what is it? What is the Mind that Dōgen Zenji talks about? What is the Universal Mind? To join these minds together, to connect our mind and the Mind of the universe is what sesshin means. We do zazen. And in zazen, we realize the oneness of such Mind. We identify ourselves with the Universal Mind, the Buddha Mind. That is what sesshin means.

Then again, we transmit, we receive, we become really aware of this state of identity of our mind, of our existence itself, and the existence of everything. This, too, is what sesshin means.

Another meaning of *setsu* is 'to control', 'adjust', or 'to assimilate'. Usually our conscious mind is very busy, continuously running around, like an excited monkey. That is what our mind is. Someone says something, we lean toward it, and we say: "That's a very good idea; that's a good way to practice." And then someone says something else, and we say: "Oh! That's better! Let's do that!" Thus we struggle to make even a little decision about what to do. Our conscious mind is always very unstable, and so to control and adjust it, and make it function properly, is another meaning of sesshin.

The first meaning, to connect our mind and the Mind of the universe, is rather active, and the second one, to control and assimilate our conscious mind, rather passive. The former is identifying with the Mind, that is to say, Buddha-nature or Dharma-nature, whatever you want to call it, while the latter one tends to be more quiet, calming and settling. Either way is quite all right.

The reason is simple.

Regardless of what kind of conscious state we have as our mind, actually that mind is already united with everything, joined with everything, one with everything. That's what we say: "All sentient beings are originally Buddhas." And since we are originally Buddhas, we are in the state of the Buddha-mind already.

What we should do is to just let it be.

What keeps that Buddha-mind from functioning as Buddha-mind is our ego-centered consciousness. Because of ego-consciousness, which is a very partial, limited, uncontrolled, unadjusted mind, we have trouble. And to try to calm this wild unadjusted mind, that is what sesshin means.

Perhaps this illustration will help us see our true mind more clearly —(laughing). It is a funny expression to say "true mind" or "false mind," but our real life, our real being itself, is itself the truth.

It could be compared with the full moon shining brightly above. The discriminative, discursive, self-conscious, self-centered thoughts which we think are our mind, are like waves on the surface of a pond. When the water is very calm and still, the moon reflects clearly upon the water. If we do not have self-oriented ideas, thoughts, the surface of our mind, of our life, is calm and clear. Then we see the moon, which is our Mind, our true being, our true life, very clearly upon the water. See?

Look at it this way. All of us, without exception, regardless of who we are, are in the midst of the Buddha-mind. In fact, simply speaking we are the Buddha-mind itself. "In the midst" is unnecessary. It is a plain fact. That is the fact that Buddha realized when he attained enlightenment. But somehow, for us, we cannot simply take it as a fact. If we take it as a fact, fine, very fine, nothing is better than that! Then just live life like that. You will have no trouble, and you'll make no trouble for others, either. But unfortunately we cannot take this very fact as it is, and again it is because of our self-oriented ideas, thoughts.

Somehow we believe this "I" exists, which is different from other things, from other people. "I" want to do such and such—"I" don't like such and such—"I" think such and such—and then, right there, the problems start. In other words, the surface of our mind becomes wavy, and even though the moon is reflected, it is distorted by the rippled surface of the water. That is your life itself. Even though you are the very fact itself, you cannot accept it, because you distort the fact by your own preoccupied thoughts, ideas.

By having sesshin, what we try to do is to see through all these troublesome illusions and delusions arising from the idea of ego or "I"-consciousness. We try to realize that ego-consciousness is a false state. We should endeavor to recognize the fact of existence. That is what sesshin means.

In sesshin, we concentrate in certain ways, and try to calm down, to make the surface of our consciousness very calm and let the facts reflect upon it clearly. Then our life gets better, easier, more comfortable, more pleasant. But what we tend to do is not only to mix ourselves up, but also to create trouble for other people, and that is really a pitiful shame.

Let's go back to the first implication of sesshin: to join, to unite, or to connect the mind. In one sense, actually we can say that everything is Mind, and Mind is the very being of Buddha-nature. We can even say Buddha itself. Nothing can exist by itself. See? It is all joined together.

For example, our lives are defined by human interrelations. It is even nonsensical to think that one can exist all by himself. Even if you crawl into a deep mountain cave, you still have connections with others. You have connections to your parents, your relatives, your friends. You have all kinds of connections with other people, regardless of how or where you live. It is like the mesh or nexuses of a net.

A net consists of many nexuses existing not independently but in the context of the other nexuses linked with it. Each nexus has four strands, and only in reference to them can that nexus exist. Our life is the same. Each individual is supported by the others, and when one nexus is broken, the entire net is weakened.

In order to emphasize the significance of the individual as a unit of a family or a society, perhaps another analogy would be helpful. Each of us is like a nexus in a net. Each one of us is, however, also the very core of the universe. You are the very center of the universe, the very, very center of life itself. So that if you do not live right, practically everything is spoiled.

Think of a balloon. With even the tiniest prick of a needle, the balloon is broken instantly. Life is the same thing; if you don't actually realize what life really is, then you completely spoil it. And by having sesshin, we try to realize what our life is. That is the meaning of sesshin.

All these different words indicate slightly different approaches to it. But the point is always the same: to realize and to actualize the ideal state of mind.

I say "mind" as if ignoring the body, but actually mind and body are the same thing. Even though we generally speak of them as two different entities, really they are one.

So to have sesshin means to have the chance to really concentrate, to realize who we really are. This is a kind of general, simple explanation of what sesshin is.

Next let us examine, practically speaking, what kind of activities are involved, what kind of schedule, what kind of ideas we are supposed to understand in order to make our sesshin together more effective.

The most important thing, the fundamental principle of sesshin is the realization and actualization of harmony.

But harmony cannot exist without the state of maintaining balance. And to maintain balance necessarily involves two or more things. On the individual level, we try to maintain the balance between body and mind so that harmony is established. And on the group level, when forty or fifty people get together to try individually to balance body and mind, then group harmony can be established.

Here, for example, we have monthly sesshin with up to fifty people attending. So these fifty people get together and try to be really harmonious. In doing this, we strongly emphasize doing things together; that is one way to help each other realize a harmonious condition. This attitude of course, must pervade all the daily activities, even extending into the hours of sleep.

SLEEP. Sesshin practice is a 24-hour practice; it does not end at the end of the day. Thus, when we go to bed at night, we try to do it harmoniously. This means that when the day is over and the lights are out, everyone just goes to bed. It is not necessary to stay up to chat or read or take walks; we simply harmonize with whatever activity is scheduled, and do it together. It is the same when morning comes. Those whose duties require it may have to get up a little early, but everybody else should simply remain in bed and rest quietly until the person in charge rings the wake-up bell. When the bell rings, just get up, put away the bedding, and be ready to begin the day's sitting. It is very simple; no one need debate with himself over sleeping a few minutes more or less. We just do what is to be done. This is the way of harmony.

SERVICES. Occasionally people question the need for rituals, chanting, and forms. It is very important to understand clearly the significance of this kind of practice.

There are two ways of looking at rituals. On the one hand, rituals are an external expression of our inner state. And on the other hand, we strengthen and reinforce our inner state by these external actions. Of course, in reality there are not two separate aspects to consider, but rather a unified whole. And as we practice together sincerely, we become increasingly aware that such terms as internal and external cannot be separated. This awareness is actually the growing realization of the real harmony which underlies everything. We are in the zendo together, and we see the altar, and we hear each other chanting, and we move together in bowing and in kinhin; this is our harmonious environment. But at the same time, because we are doing these things and concentrating on what we are doing, this is our harmonious consciousness. Our environment and our consciousness are inseparable. The two are one.

In this perspective, we can see that even such details as the clothes we wear in the zendo are extremely significant in achieving this harmonious practice. What we are doing is important enough that we must consider our appearance. If there is too much informality in dress, then the group practice may be somewhat disturbed. Such clothing as shorts or undershirts seems out of place in the zendo. Bright colors or strong perfumes, jewelry that jingles, all these may in themselves be quite all right, even attractive, but because our practice in the zendo is one of group harmony, they prove to be distractions and not helpful to the other people present.

Some people complain, "I don't like to chant." Such a complaint indicates nothing but disharmony within oneself. The body cannot really participate fully because the small mind, the discursive, ego-conscious mind, does not "want" to. This is not the way to practice, though. When we have services, we simply have services. We must be in harmony within the individual, within the group, and within the atmosphere. The secret, the key to this harmony, is simply to be selfless. It always comes back to this point—the self. If you are self-centered you spoil everything, but if you are selfless everything goes smoothly. In accord with the schedule and character of these activities, we do things in certain ways. All that is necessary is just to fit in with these ways, to follow and be harmonious.

CHANTING. Chanting is an effective means of harmonizing body and mind. It should not be shouting, as some people do. When they shout, it is distracting. When a person chants like this, he chants as if only he exists and no one else, which is not so. Chant with your ears, not with your mouth. When chanting, be aware of the others who are also chanting. Blend your voice with their voices. Make one voice, all together. We say, "Chant not too high, not too low, not too fast, not too slow." Take your pace from the senior monk, who will take the initiative. Always adjust yourself to the others, rather than expecting them to adjust to you. Then there is harmony. We say, "Chant as though each syllable were a drop of rain in a steady shower." It is very mild, consistent, and sustained. "Kanjizaibosagyojinhannyaharamitajishoken-goun . . ."

Chanting functions the same as all of our practices. On one level, we can see that the sutras we chant have their own content; they mean something. Some, like the *Heart Sutra* for example, are especially concise and packed with deep meaning. But again, apart from the texts, the act of chanting is in itself an absolute practice, simultaneously expressing and creating an inner state of consciousness. And as we chant together and hear each other chanting, we are helped further in joining our minds. This is harmony. This is sesshin.

KINHIN. Sometimes after the sitting period ends, some people wish to continue to sit on their cushions during kinhin. Of course, if you are very deeply absorbed in your samadhi, you may not realize that the bell has rung, or you may even be unable to move. Then it is all right to remain seated. But if you hear the bell ring, it is better to do kinhin with everyone else.

When the sitting period ends and we begin to do kinhin, we should try to avoid making the transition from sitting to walking too abrupt. Kinhin is simply another way to do zazen; so it should be as smooth and harmonious as our breathing. Just as the transition from inhaling to exhaling must be very easy and continuous, so it is with kinhin.

Sitting, standing, bowing, walking, whatever we do, if we are careful to maintain mindfulness, we can always be sitting, always be in harmony. But if we hear the bell signaling the end of zazen and suddenly break concentration we make our practice loose and weak.

TENZO. It would be a mistake to think that the purpose of the kitchen and its staff is simply to prepare meals. Of course, that is one part of kitchen practice, the most obvious part perhaps, but there is far more to it than that.

We can say that without food there is no life, and without life, no practice. And we know that since each of us is the Buddha, those working in the kitchen are supporting the life of the Buddha. That is one way to see the content of kitchen practice. But also, as with sutras and chanting, the act is an absolute practice in and of itself. The kitchen is a continuous testing-ground. From moment to moment there is so much to be done; conditions are always changing. And everything can be done in so many ways! How do we slice the vegetables? How do we scrub the utensils? At every turn we express our inner state: by sloppiness, by being meticulous, by avoiding work or seeking it, concentrating or daydreaming, being calm or tense, and so on. It is not an easy matter to remain mindful and unconditioned under the pressure of a busy kitchen. But if this is a challenging practice, it is also potentially a very rewarding one.

Arising out of the individual's own inner state is the collective harmony (or lack of it) of the kitchen staff. And from this arises the harmony of kitchen and zendo. We say, "kitchen and zendo," but this is only a manner of speaking. They are not really two entities even if physically separate. Certainly a loosely-operating kitchen, with unnecessary chatter and sloppiness, makes a very definite impact on the rest of the zendo. As the servers move between kitchen and zendo, the proper concentration and silence as well as the overall continuity of mood express a oneness, a harmony that is also sesshin.

ORYOKI. I would like to deal briefly with the oryoki. It is so significant that to go into it thoroughly would take a great deal of time. But at least we can appreciate some very fundamental aspects of it. When we eat our meals during sesshin, we use a set of nested bowls, the largest of which is called the Buddha-bowl or oryoki. In the sutras we chant before meals, we approximately translate oryoki as "Buddha Tathagata's eating bowls." But the oryoki is not just the bowl provided by the zendo. The Buddha Tathagata's eating bowl is your bowl. You are the Buddha, eating from the bowl of the Buddha. Realize this fact.

In the original Chinese, it does not quite say "eating bowls." Just oryoki, which literally means a container which holds just the necessary amount. That is what it means, no more, no less. That is existence, life itself.

Some people need more food than others; your need is not necessarily in proportion to your body weight. But these individual differences are all right. Some take more, others less. It is simply the operation of natural balance.

But we need not think that we are speaking only of eating bowls when we mention oryoki. More fundamentally, oryoki is just the Tathagata's container. We can appreciate everything as the container of the Buddha. We are oryoki ourselves. Not only us, but Buddha's image, candle holders, vase, bowing mat, floor, ceiling—each contains everything completely. It is all oryoki. The whole universe itself is the container of the Buddha Tathagata.

This is our bowl. And this is the bowl from which we eat and maintain our life. So that as we become more aware of this fact, we will appreciate life more. We eat food. But what is our food? It is the Buddha too. That is to say, it is life, giving life to life. Again here is total harmony, and that is the way of existence. When we eat, we had better be aware of at least these facts.

It is a very important part of sesshin too, to realize how significant our life is, our actions are. Even when we go to the restroom we should be very careful. Dōgen Zenji set forth very detailed instructions in the Shōbōgenzō; he virtually spelled out every waking moment of the day for careful practice. Of course, at this stage in our practice it is too much for us to go into too fully just yet, so we do not emphasize all these details right away. But when you become aware of yourself—or rather, simply when you become aware—you become meticulous. The more your awareness grows, the more careful you grow. It is a very natural thing. Then if your actions are sloppy, your understanding is sloppy, your life is sloppy, and everything is sloppy.

But here in sesshin, we try not to be so, and we try to realize the very significant, subtle meaning of our life. That is what we are trying to do here. And in studying ourselves, we find the harmony that is our total existence. We do not make harmony. We do not achieve or gain it. It is there all the time. Here we are, in the midst of this perfect way, and our practice is simply to realize it and then, to actualize it in our everyday life.

All day long, we are living the life of the Buddha. Opening oryoki, we look into the Buddha. Functioning in every way, we are in the midst of the operation of the Dharma. It is all us. We are all it. And this inseparable unity is the Sangha.

CHAPTER 4

A PORTRAIT OF SESSHIN
Photography by Paul Turner

Sesshin is a one-week intensive training period. Throughout the six-and-a-half days, the cycle of zazen, instruction, service, meals and work repeats itself. Each day's schedule is a duplicate of the one before it and the one after it. But because the participants are moving continuously deeper into themselves, and because their awareness of the group's practice is continually expanding, the experience is one of newness and depth rather than mere repetition.

DAILY SESSHIN SCHEDULE

4:00	Wake-up
4:30–6:30	Dawn Zazen with Dokusan
6:30–7:00	Morning Service
7:00–7:40	Breakfast
7:40–8:00	Wash, Prepare for Samu
8:00–9:10	Samu
9:10–9:30	Clean-up, Prepare for Zazen
9:30–11:30	Morning Zazen with Dokusan
11:30–11:45	Mid-day Service
11:45–12:30	Lunch
12:30–2:00	Free Sitting, Rest, Exercise
2:00–2:30	Zazen
2:30–3:30	Teisho
3:30–4:30	Zazen
4:30–4:45	Evening Service
4:45–5:30	Supper
5:30–6:30	Free Sitting, Rest, Exercise
6:30–9:00	Evening Zazen with Dokusan
9:30	Lights Out

Learning how to use the eating bowls

Zazen

In the early 20th Century, Daiun Harada
Roshi started a series of comprehensive
introductory lectures to orient new
students. This series has been continued
by many of his successors. At ZCLA it is
presented in the American idiom.

During zazen the sitters are monitored
by a senior student who can correct
posture and offer encouragement and
stimulation by the use of a flattened
stick.

At various times, the Roshi inspects the Zendo, ascertaining the overall atmosphere as well as the individual posture and bearing.

Waiting to see their teacher for individual guidance (dokusan), students maintain unbroken concentration.

As the teacher's bell signals readiness, the
student responds in kind with two
rings on the dokusan bell and enters the
teacher's private room.

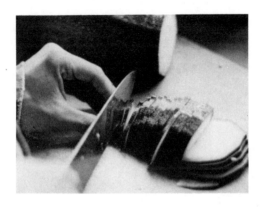

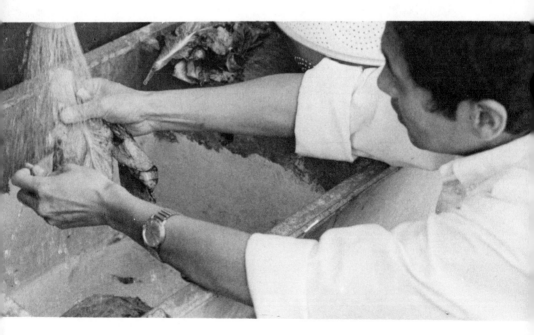

To minimize talking and aid concentration, scheduled activities are signalled by a variety of percussion instruments.

Roshi's formal commentary (teisho) on Zen texts is begun and ended by chanting verses to enhance appreciation of what is received.

By mid-sesshin, the momentum of steady practice often carries students through rest periods as they remain in deep concentration day and night.

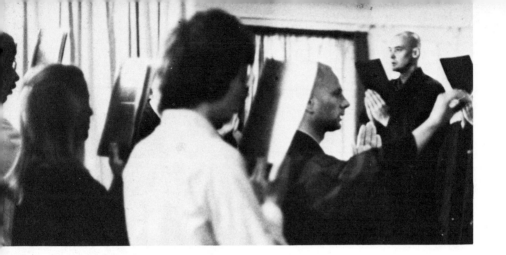

In services, participants express gratitude and appreciation of their true nature.

Great Release—After an effortful week, students emerge from the Zendo into a world which is unchanged and yet totally different.

CHAPTER 5

NOTES ON KOAN STUDY
Bernard Tetsugen Glassman

I'd like to spend this evening talking about koan study, and then have some time at the end for questions and answers. Approximately one-third of the people studying under Maezumi Roshi are working on koans. Normally, Roshi's teishos are about various koan collections. But we haven't had many general talks about koan study, as a study.

As it exists now, there are two basic koan systems. One was organized by Master Inzan, the other by Master Takuju. Inzan and Takuju were two Zen masters in Japan. In the Dharma lineage they were grandsons of Hakuin Zenji.

Hakuin Zenji is responsible for organizing koan study as we know it today. He has an amazing autobiography, and I recommend everybody read it. [1] He was born in 1686 and died in 1769. He studied under various masters, studying various koan systems. Each master had his own way of handling koans. And by the use of koans, Hakuin sharpened his understanding and had many kensho experiences. In his autobiography he talks about them.

Hakuin was very impressed with the use of koans and zazen to deepen understanding. So as a teacher, he very strongly emphasized zazen and koan study. And having studied under so many different teachers, having seen so many different styles, he felt it best to organize the koans into a system by which one could refine his understanding. He himself never completed that organization. But two of his grandsons in the Dharma did finish organizing these koans into two systems.

---

1. Selections from Hakuin Zenji's autobiography appear in *A History of Zen Buddhism*, by Heinrich Dumoulin, *The Embossed Tea Kettle*, translated by R.D.M. Shaw, and *The Zen Master Hakuin*, by Philip Yampolsky.

Hakuin had over ninety Dharma successors. He is of the Rinzai sect. And in Japan, after Hakuin, the Rinzai sect flourished very strongly. One of his successors, Gasan Jito, continued Hakuin's work of organizing the koan study. Then the two roshis that I mentioned, Inzan and Takuju, both disciples of Gasan, finished the organization of the koan system as we know it today.

Inzan and Takuju had completely different personalities. Inzan was very vigorous, very dynamic. Takuju was very meticulous, very careful in his study. And two koan systems developed, having the characteristics of the two teachers: one system being a very dynamic system, and the other forcing you to be very meticulous with each koan, with each point of each koan.

Yasutani Roshi is in the Takuju line, stressing the meticulous examination of the koans. Kōryū Roshi is in the Inzan line, stressing the dynamic interpretation of the koans. Maezumi Roshi, as you know, received Inka from both Yasutani Roshi and Kōryū Roshi, and studied both lines. So in a way, we can say he is similar to Hakuin Zenji. Both, in their day, studied with various masters and different methods, and both developed a system which they felt applicable for their time.

Koans existed before Hakuin Zenji; they go back to the time of Shakyamuni Buddha. The flavor of koans in India is different from the flavor of koans in China, and is different from the flavor of koans developed in Japan. And definitely, there will be koans and koan systems developed in this country. The flavor will be somewhat different, but I personally think that any koan system which develops here should include koans dealing with all these periods of time.

Koans originally developed out of daily life with the students themselves. The student came to a place to study and brought with him a question—his own koan. But usually, if we look at the students who brought their own koans, and persisted in examining their own koans until they came to a resolution, those students stick out as being fine roshis or exceptional students. That is, the average person does not persist in the question that pops up during his daily life. He doesn't work on it with the vigor and passion that's demanded in order to break through this dichotomy.

So as the number of students began to increase, the Patriarchs, masters and roshis would give koans to the students as a technique to force them to penetrate—to go further than where they were—to shatter the dichotomy.

Generally, koans formed two categories. The first, a koan we work on before the first opening—before this first breakthrough—and the second, the koans we work on after this first breakthrough.

Shakyamuni Buddha worked, sat, practiced for many years before his enlightenment experience. In his case, that enlightenment experience was extremely deep. But in general, the first experience is more like poking a hole in the wall. So, we study further to enlarge that hole and finally to break apart that wall.

Due to the compassion of the Patriarchs and masters, koan study developed into an extremely intricate, detailed study. The first series of koans that we use to produce the first opening gives us a glimpse of the Dharmakaya, of sunyata, of emptiness, of Buddha-nature.

Then we study koans called the Hosshin, or Dharmakaya koans, until you feel at home in this world of emptiness, until the Dharmakaya is completely familiar to you—the world of Oneness. Many people, having some sort of experience of this Oneness, get stuck there. They think that's it. They experience the Oneness of all things, feel completely at home with themselves, with Buddha, with the state of *I am.* But staying there is no good. That's *makyo.* [2]

Next, we study Kikan koans. We examine the differentiation, the differences. Everything is different. But we have to see these differences from the position of Oneness. Everything is the same, but at the same time, everything is different.

Then, completely understanding the Oneness of life, the Buddha; completely understanding the differences, the Dharma—then, we study the Gonsen koans. We learn how to use words to express this understanding. In a way, this is a very difficult, very important part of koan study. We read in books that enlightenment can't be described, can't be talked about—that wisdom, prajna, can't be expressed. But we have to learn how to express it. As humans, we communicate, we relate.

2. *makyo:* In general, anything to which we become attached.

After we have studied koans from many different angles, we then investigate the *Gōi* koans—the Five Positions[3] of Tōzan Zenji. Tōzan was the founder of the Soto sect, and he developed what's called the Five Positions—*Gōi*. In the koan system, they're used both as a summary of the five stages of our practice and as a detailed examination of the absolute and the relative. And in koan study, we examine each of these Five Positions and sharpen and polish up our understanding.

Then we investigate the *kai*. Many of you have had jukai—the *kai*, the aspects of the enlightened life. There are about a hundred koans dealing with these various aspects of our lives, these sixteen different *kai*.

That's the general form or structure of koan study. And if at any point along the study, or if at any point along our practice, we develop the feeling that our understanding is complete—then right there, we have trapped ourselves in a sticky web.

Along with this koan study, Hakuin Zenji developed what he called "capping phrases," *jakugo*. He used these capping phrases as a method of letting us increase our ability to express our understanding.

As they developed in Japan, these capping phrases are phrases that appear in the classical literature—one word, two words, one line, two lines, four lines. The student, after realizing the spirit and expressing the content of a koan, was asked to go to the classical literature and find a phrase expressing the spirit of the koan.[4]

Now in this country, sometimes capping phrases are also used. They originate in two ways. One, they are taken from literature (which is commonly done in Japan); two they are taken from our own words. Each has its own advantage.

In studying koans, it's important to take each koan and dissect it. Just chew it up! Let that koan become a part of our whole body—our bones, our blood. And sit with it. If we study koans in that way, then each one becomes an integral part of us.

Having studied koans in that manner, we can then make a new system, or we can add to the current system, and integrate it into our culture in a more intimate manner.

---

3. One explanation of the Five Ranks appears in chapter VII of *The Zen Koan*, by Isshu Miura Roshi and Ruth Fuller Sasaki.

4. More information on capping phrases is given in Part Three of *The Zen Koan*, Selections from a Zen Phrase Anthology.

Now, koans have to be looked at as a system and as a technique for causing our first breakthrough and for deepening it. But they're not unique, and they're not the only technique. They're not the only way of doing Zen study. But I personally feel they're extremely valuable. And it can help us to eliminate the feeling that we can sit where we are and that everything is clear to us.

Thank you.

QUESTIONS AND ANSWERS

Chiko: You were discussing the changing or developing of koan systems; that we would develop our own koans and koan systems in this country. These koans that we study seem like a dream-land in the sense that things like that just don't happen nowadays; that is, it seems like a lot of the koans are obsolete in terms of our everyday life. I just can't relate to them at all. Everyday life and work seem more like a koan for me.

Tetsugen: Now definitely, koans that come up in daily life, or things that come up in our day-to-day dealings, can be thought of as koans and dealt with as koans. In many cases, that's how original koans in our koan study have developed. But the point is, normally, when something comes up in daily life, we treat it sort of superficially. So koan study is essentially a technique to make us persist in driving home, in dealing with this question, until we fully resolve it. Now, if we did that with questions or the problems that come up in daily life, and if enough of a variety of problems came up, then we'd be creating a new kind of koan system.

It's obvious that you could learn chemistry by reading books and by experimenting. But if you go to school and take a course with a set-up lab where you have to go through various experiments—it's an aid to learning. We don't really need that crutch. We could say that those kinds of crutches aren't necessary, and certainly that's true. But the majority of us need those crutches.

I studied with Krishnamurti for a while, and as you know, he strongly recommends against a teacher. He strongly recommends against almost any kind of crutch you can think of. For him that worked out—although he had teachers too. For his personality that was appropriate. But he acts as a teacher, and the majority of us need that kind of help.

So koan systems developed as a means for Zen teachers to deal with large numbers of students. Some of their students don't need the koan system in order to drive through to the core of Zen and many students aren't simpatico to a koan system; that is, the koan system isn't applicable for everybody.

It's not enough to just say that things will come up in daily life. That's true, but we have to really work on those situations in the same way that we work on a koan system, and persist until we come up with the answer.

Also, there are lots of koans. I find, of the koans that do exist, the same things that happened in those koans are happening now. In koan study, there are episodes of happenings between various teachers and students. The enlightenment experiences of the first fifty-two Patriarchs are koans. Experiences of Shakyamuni Buddha and Dōgen Zenji are also koans, and so are other incidents that happened. If you work on those, you develop a feeling of the history of Zen through India, China, and Japan. To me an amazing thing is that even though the cultures are so different, and the way Zen manifests itself in each culture is quite different, still, I can see the same things happening in the development of Zen in this country as we can see appearing in these koans. There are koans that deal with students who, for example, travel from center to center, from place to place. You see the same exact thing here. There are koans that deal with all the aspects of life we see here.

Now, some koans have some terms that are a little strange. We're not familiar with those terms so we can replace them. Some koans have as background the culture and milieu of India or China or Japan, and perhaps that background can be replaced. But the essence of the koans, that's the same. And more than that, the historical background that the koans rest in, I think, is the same except for a change in name from Shanghai to Brooklyn.

Still, the koan system has to be modified. But the modification needed is not so basic as you suggested. The essence is really still the same, but the system will have to be modified, and it has been. It has been different in each of the cultures where Zen has flourished, and it will change here. It has to.

•

Myoko: I'd appreciate it if you'd talk more about the sequence of koan study.

Tetsugen: The sequence that I talked about is, in a way, the more orthodox, or the more general sequence. But, for example, Yasutani Roshi's way of handling koans was different and I'll explain that.

Hakuin Zenji first divided koan study into basically two types of koans: koan study before the first opening, and koan study after the first opening. There's a distinct difference in the two types of study.

In koan study before the first opening, different koans can be used. Here we work on muji, "Jōshū's mu." "The sound of one hand" is a koan originated by Hakuin Zenji and is sometimes used as the first koan. The Sixth Patriarch, Master Enō, said, "What was your original face before your parents were born?" That's also a first koan. Those are used to help us penetrate into the Dharma, the Dharmakaya, to have this first opening.

Then the next category of koans is called Hosshin koans, or the Heart of the Dharmakaya, body of the Dharma. There are about fifty to a hundred general koans that are used to help us examine this Dharmakaya, opening our eyes a little, more and more. We examine the essence of the Dharma, appreciate the oneness of life, the unity of life.

Then, seeing the oneness, standing from that position of the Absolute, look at the Relative, the relativeness of life, the differences, Understand the subtle differences. Two pieces of white paper that look exactly alike are completely different. Appreciate the differences, standing at this vantage point of the unity of life.

Then examine the intricacies of words. In Zen we say that enlightenment can't be discussed, the essence of Zen can't be talked about. It has to be realized, experienced. That's true. But it has to be discussed. So appreciate the subtle use of words. See the difference between live words and dead words. See the effect that your words have. Be careful of what we say. Words are extremely powerful things. So we study the subtleties of words. We learn how to express this unity of life, the differences of life, the Dharmakaya.

Then we examine the Five Positions of Tōzan Zenji, the master who founded the Soto Sect. These Five Positions are looking at: 1) the Absolute within the Relative, 2) the Relative within the Absolute, 3) the Absolute, 4) the Relative, and 5) undifferentiated Oneness. Essentially, the Five Positions is a summary of our practice. Generally, I think about fifty koans are used to examine these Five Positions.

Then we deal with the *kai*. That's generally the trend of koan study.

Now, in Yasutani Roshi's system, we first study about a hundred koans dealing with these general subjects. Then we look at various koan collections and go in order in those books. So it gets a little mixed up, because some of these koans are dealing with some subjects and some with others. It's not in any particular order anymore.

The Roshi deals with each student individually, using those koans. Normally, what he does is to see where you're stuck and not quite aware of it. When he deals with you with those koans, he forces you to look at them from the vantage point of eliminating the places you're hanging onto. So different people study the same koan very differently because they're sticking to different places.

The books that we study in Yasutani Roshi's system are the *Mumonkan (Gateless Gate)*, which has forty-eight cases; the *Hekigan roku (Blue Cliff Record)*, which has a hundred cases, and then the *Shōyō roku (Book of Equanimity)*, which has a hundred cases also. Maezumi Roshi is giving teishos on that and we're appreciating the cases in sesshin now. Then we next study the *Denko roku*, which is a collection of the enlightenment experiences of the first fifty-one Patriarchs plus Shakyamuni Buddha. So that's fifty-two cases.

The *Denko roku* was compiled by Keizan Zenji, the Fourth Patriarch of the Soto Sect in Japan. He lived three generations of Dharma succession after Dōgen Zenji. Keizan Zenji is actually mainly responsible for the spreading of the Soto Sect in Japan.

The *Denko roku* starts with Shakyamuni Buddha's enlightenment experience and then goes through the enlightenment experiences of each of the Patriarchs; Mahakashapa, Ananda, and so forth. We chant the names of these Patriarchs in our morning service. Keizan Zenji wrote a poem on each enlightenment experience, expressing his understanding of that experience. In our koan study, we appreciate those. So that's another fifty-two cases.

Then we appreciate Master Tōzan's *Gōi*, the Five Positions, and then the precepts, the sixteen *kai*. It's a very comprehensive study, and normally we are such that we wouldn't be that comprehensive with ourselves.

•

Julie: Do you have any ideas on what kind of personalities should not study koans?

Tetsugen: Those who don't want to study them.

•

Kakushin: Before koan study became a system, I suppose there was a spontaneous kind of koan system in existence, depending on the person, where he was, or his problem at the time, or . . .

Tetsugen: Yes, there was. We talk about the koan system as we know it now, as going back to Hakuin Zenji. He formalized it as a training method. In his time, he studied koans when he was given koans to study. We could go way back in history to find people who were given koans to study, but it wasn't a comprehensive system the way Hakuin Zenji did it. Hakuin felt very strongly that a number of students who were studying Zen were not pressing as far as he felt they should, that people were stopping at different places. He himself studied very strongly. He studied with a lot of teachers and had lots of experiences. He insisted that the monks who studied at his monastery practice very hard and go very deep. He built up this koan system to keep them going so that they couldn't stop, and he made a very comprehensive system. He was motivated to do that because of the number of students who wanted to study, and the feeling he had that they needed something to keep them going, so that they didn't stop at some point. But definitely, before him, there were koans given out, and there were also different systems.

There was one Zen master who used one koan as his koan system, one I particularly like: "Sitting on top of a hundred-foot pole, how do you go one step further?" Now, he'd use that when a student first came, and then, when the student passed that koan, he'd give it back to him. That's a particularly nice one to use for that purpose, because we're always on top of that hundred-foot pole, and we always have to go one foot further.[5] There were, as you say, lots of students who came to a teacher with their own koan and asked a question, and then worked at that.

Kakushin: I was thinking of what Chiko said. What I heard her say is that she doesn't seem to feel the koans are answering her particular problems at the present time. I was wondering if maybe those problems could become her koan. Is there any way of doing that?

Tetsugen: Sure! Sure.

Kakushin: Could you effectively work on that kind of basis?

Tetsugen: Sure. As you said, originally, that's how they developed. The point is that koans—muji as a specific example—are very valuable, because they help to eliminate, very quickly, the use of the intellect in breaking through this first barrier. Some questions that pop up in daily life tend to emphasize the use of the intellect. Using them could be much harder and take much longer to break through than using something like muji, but if you're strongly motivated by something that happens, and motivated enough to keep working at it, definitely, that's of stronger value. Yet, a lot of times, with those things that pop up in daily life, that strong motivation that we have . . . next week, we don't have such a strong motivation for it. Because there is a big intellectual flavor to it, we get tired of working on it, and you don't pound into it. It's not as easy to dig in as it is with "Jōshū's mu."

---

5. The koan referred to here is listed as Case 46 of *The Gateless Gate.*

CHAPTER 6

"BODHIDHARMA'S PACIFYING THE MIND"
The Gateless Gate, Case 41
Kōryū Osaka Roshi
Translated by Peter Kakuzen Gregory

The Gateless Gate or *Mumonkan* is the most popular and widely used of all Zen koan collections. In 1228 AD, the Chinese Rinzai Zen Master Mumon Ekai (1183-1260) selected forty-eight important koans from the sayings of the old masters, added his own commentary and verse to each one, and gave them to his students for their Zen study. The *Mumonkan* was first brought to Japan in 1254 AD by one of Mumon's disciples, the Japanese monk Shinji Kakushin (1207-1298). The first case of the *Mumonkan*, and one of the most famous, is "Jōshū's mu," on which Master Mumon worked for six years before attaining enlightenment. This forty-first case concerns an event that occurred between the First and Second Chinese Zen Patriarchs in the sixth century AD.

MAIN CASE:

Bodhidharma sat facing the wall. The Second Patriarch stood outside in the snow. He cut off his arm and said: "My mind is not yet at peace. Please, Master, put my mind at ease." Bodhidharma said: "Bring me your mind and I will pacify it for you." The Second Patriarch replied: "Although I have searched for the mind, it is utterly ungraspable." Bodhidharma said: "Then I have pacified your mind for you."

MUMON'S COMMENTARY:

The broken-toothed old barbarian proudly came 100,000 *li* across the sea. It could be said that this was raising waves without any wind. In the end, he had only one disciple, and even he was a cripple. Alas! Shasanrō doesn't even know four characters.

MUMON'S VERSE:

Coming from the west and directly pointing—
The affairs are caused by the transmission.
The trouble-maker for Zen monasteries
Is, after all, you.

Today's koan is Case 41 of *The Gateless Gate*, "Bodhidharma's Pacifying the Mind." Since we are already on the forty-first case and *The Gateless Gate* only contains forty-eight cases, next month we should just about be finished. Indeed it goes fast.

Many are the days and months spent idly,
But few indeed are the hours for seeking the Dharma.

Time passes by quickly and we grow old before we realize it.

Since all of you are working, naturally it's impossible for you just to concentrate on your practice. However, since the standpoint of our practice is based on the principle that we must continue to polish and

1. I would appreciate a subscription to *ZEN WRITINGS* series (2 volumes per year).

1 year U.S.	$7 ☐	2 year U.S. $13 ☐
1 year foreign	$9 ☐	2 year foreign $17 ☐

2. Please send me the back volume(s)

ZCLA JOURNAL:	"On Science and Zen"	$3 ☐
	"Yasutani Roshi Memorial Issue"	$3 ☐
ZEN WRITINGS:	*ON ZEN PRACTICE, 2nd edition*	$4 ☐

3. Please send me information about the Zen Center of Los Angeles

Name _____

Address _____

City _____

State _____ Zip _____

To help us save postage and handling costs, please enclose a check or money order with this card and send to:

Zen Center of Los Angeles
927 South Normandie
Los Angeles, California 90006

refine ourselves in the midst of our work, we can't say that we are unable to practice because of our work.

Coming to a *dōjō* like this is a good opportunity for extending your practice to your work. Sitting—or doing zazen—is the easiest place to begin. You should carry the spirit of doing zazen over to your work. Since we emphasize the proper disposition of body, spirit, and mind even at your work, if you can't do it properly at the *dōjō*, then it will be even harder to do it at work. If you first make a habit of doing it properly where it is easy to do it and then extend this to your work you'll be able to do it throughout the rest of your life. When you do this, your life, work, business, and everyday activity will be vitalized. Otherwise, it's meaningless.

First of all, you should make your life genuine. Then you can with your own body and mind fully and directly appreciate the significance and joy of life, the happiness of really living, and you will be able to delight in others. This is what I mean by "the taste of Zen."

You should try to see how you can apply this spirit of *dōjō* practice to your work and then endeavor to put it into practice. As you progress, you come to appreciate more and more the true joy and meaningfulness of living. No matter how long it takes, it's all right, just as long as you realize this.

This is something that anyone can realize. It will definitely come about as a result of your own earnestness and effort. If it takes a long time, try and see why it's taking a long time. Since it is easiest to do at the *dōjō*, you should just throw yourself totally into it without holding anything back. When you do this, your limitations will gradually decrease and your capabilities will become stronger. As a result, a turnabout takes place.

Today's case is one of the most important koans for Zen as it deals with Bodhidharma's coming to China and transmitting the Dharma to the Second Patriarch, Master Eka.

Bodhidharma is very familiar to the Japanese. Although some scholars doubt his historical existence, even Japanese children have a clear image of him. Although he had such a tremendous impact on China and Japan, he was an Indian, the third son of the ruler of a kingdom in Southern India.

Bodhidharma

Scroll painting by Shōun Tomiyama

The ruler of this kingdom was a man who had a strong aspiration to practice the Way. Bodhidharma's teacher, Hannyatara, was the twenty-seventh successor of the Dharma from Shakyamuni. He was frequently invited to the palace to expound the Dharma, for which the king was extremely grateful.

Once, when Hannyatara and his attendant were invited there to chant sutras, only the attendant chanted, while Hannyatara did not. Even though he wasn't asleep, his voice couldn't be heard. Later, when he was asked about it, he replied that he was concentrating on his breathing. When he exhaled, he became one with the exhalation and when he inhaled, he became one with his inhalation. In this way he was expounding the Dharma. Since he had practiced breathing as it should have been practiced, it was the same as chanting the sutras the way they should have been chanted.

If you can totally just follow your breath, then each breath becomes the vital activity of life. Since the master was following his breath perfectly, he was expounding the Dharma exactly as it should be expounded.

The king was deeply impressed and presented a splendid jewel to Hannyatara. Hannyatara used it to test the princes. The first and second sons praised it, saying that such a splendid gem could only be possessed by their father, the king. However, the third son, Bodhitara, said that although it was splendid, the true jewel was not a material thing, but the mind. He said that a material jewel only gives off worldly light, but that the true light is the light of wisdom. Such a statement, which we might expect a philosopher or religious genius to make, was made by Bodhidharma when he was only seven years old.

Hannyatara was greatly impressed and said that this third son would be a great man in the future and kept a close watch on Bodhidharma from childhood on. When the king died, Bodhidharma meditated for a solid week before his coffin and entered into a deep state of samadhi; he said that he wanted to become a disciple of Hannyatara. At that time Hannyatara said, "You have already innately penetrated all dharmas and true reality."

This kind of wisdom is called "innate wisdom." Since Bodhitara

was such an exceptional person, Hannyatara renamed him Bodhidharma
—"dharma" means penetrating everything.

He served Hannyatara for forty years after that. After Hannyatara
died, he propagated Buddhism for sixty-seven years, against the six
schools of ancient Indian philosophy. Since Bodhidharma began studying with Hannyatara when he was about ten-years-old, he must have
been around fifty when Hannyatara died; if we add another sixty-seven
years to this, he must have been over 110. It was at this age that he left
for China. As there was the famous overland trade route known as the
silk road, one of our members said that there must also have been an
ocean silk road—at any rate, Bodhidharma came to China by boat. Even
though we can travel to the moon today, in the period when Bodhidharma lived, some 1500 years ago, crossing 100,000 *li* of rough seas
coming from India to China was no small feat. Presumably, he met with
a number of setbacks but finally, after three years, he reached Hong
Kong. He sailed up the Pearl River and landed at present-day Canton.
He stayed there for a short while building a small hermitage called
"Coming-from-the-West Hut."

Soon after this, the governor reported to Emperor Wu of Liang
that a wonderful old priest had arrived from India. Consequently, Emperor Wu invited Bodhidharma to his court—their meeting is recorded
as the first case of *The Blue Cliff Records.* Although Emperor Wu was
known as "Buddha-Mind Son of Heaven," he couldn't understand
Bodhidharma's essential spirit. Later, he exclaimed: "Even though I met
him, I didn't meet him"—even though he had seen Bodhidharma's super-
ficial appearance, he had been unable to penetrate his true spirit. "Both
now and before—I rue it, I regret it." Thus, although the Emperor met
him, he was unable to meet the True Man and so lost the chance of a
thousand years. At any rate, the daughter of Emperor Wu went to study
with Bodhidharma and eventually succeeded his Dharma.'

Because Emperor Wu of Liang didn't understand, Bodhidharma
crossed the Yangtse River and went to the Shao-lin temple in the kingdom of Wei. Up until that time, many monks came and stayed there.
He didn't build his own temple, but stayed in a cave-like place and did
zazen for nine years. He didn't do this for his own sake, but (in order)
to wait for the right person to come.

Eventually, the Second Patriarch, Master Eka (Hui-k'o) came there. He was a wonderful person and was called "Divine Light" (Shinkō) because a dazzling light had shone in the room where he was born. He had studied Confucianism and Taoism and was well-learned and advanced in practice.

Even though Bodhidharma's just doing zazen may seem to be somewhat passive, I think that in the case of someone like Bodhidharma sitting there like· that, he must have been sending out wonderful vibrations from his body-mind which were more powerful than those of a huge broadcasting station. His aura radiated these vibrations just like the radiation of uranium. For one of such repeated tempering and discipline as Bodhidharma, just sitting there, he must have really emanated amazing vibrations. And so, just as television waves are received, his disciples began to tune into his frequency. When they synchronized onto the same wavelength, a wonderful resonance began to build up. At first, even though Bodhidharma was there, their response was slight; but it increased continually, attracting his disciples one after the other.

> Peaches and plums don't talk, and yet
> The path is naturally made under their blossoms.

Shinkō Eka Daishi was the first of the disciples to be drawn there, and although he had done so at great difficulty, Bodhidharma just sat facing the wall of his cave. Even though Eka announced his purpose, Bodhidharma just continued sitting, without greeting him. Eka just stood there. It was the night of December ninth and a heavy snow fell. The snow didn't fall on Bodhidharma, but since the Second Patriarch Eka Daishi was standing outside, the snow gradually piled up, burying his legs. Severe as Bodhidharma was, finally he said: "You there, standing in the snow, what do you want?" Feeling relieved, Eka entreated Bodhidharma to save all deluded beings. But Bodhidharma admonished him: "The unsurpassable subtle Way of all Buddhas is unattainable unless you devote all your spiritual energy and effort to it over an extremely long period of time. You can never accomplish it unless you are a man who can practice what is difficult to practice and bear what is difficult to bear. Even if you try that hard, you will only be able to realize a little. With your careless and conceited mind, you already feel as if you control all under heaven and want to trifle with it—with such an easy-going attitude, you'll never be able to accomplish the Buddha Way."

Knowing this quite well, the Second Patriarch Master Eka, in order to show the strength of his resolution, cut off his left arm with the sword that he was carrying and presented his amputated arm gushing blood onto the pure white snow.

At that, Bodhidharma said, "Those who in the past have truly searched for the Dharma have never given a thought to their own physical well-being. Since you have such determination, you have the capacity to accomplish it, and it is fitting that you do so." When Bodhidharma asked his reason for striving with such determination, Eka pleaded, "My mind is in upheaval and I can gain no repose. Please, put my mind at ease." When Bodhidharma said, "Then bring me your mind and I will pacify it for you," his problem had solidified.

While he was thinking that his mind was disturbed, he couldn't simply bring it forward. Thus, in the end, he saw deeply into his own mind.

Among you doing zazen idly or even working on the koan muji, there are many of you who don't know how to do it. Although it's not easy to understand at first, as I always say, straighten up your posture and with a correctly aligned body, properly sit. With steadfast resolution, sit massively. When you do so, then as the body becomes correctly positioned, the *hara*[1] also begins to sit. When the hara sits, when you physically and mentally center your breathing in the *tanden* and *kikai*, then you don't think about Jōshū's muji up in your head. This mu is without a doubt the wonderful truth. Even though you have questions like what kind of principle is in this muji or why muji has become such an important theme, you should just continue to investigate them persistently, muing with your *tanden* and *kikai*. With all your guts, just exhaust every ounce of your mental, physical and spiritual energy in muji. Concentrate. Concentrate. Don't split your attention up. Just continue to squeeze everything out with all you've got.

---

1. *hara*: The region of the lower abdomen comprising *tanden* and *kikai*; cf. p.94.

When you just continue like this with all your guts, then no matter how tired you become, no matter how much your legs hurt, and no matter how many disturbances you have, just continue "mu" single-mindedly. When thoughts about things that you did yesterday or have to do tomorrow spring up in your mind, even though all kinds of thoughts may occur, don't pay them any mind; just let them be and they will reinforce your single-minded concentration on muji.

What you couldn't do at first, you begin to be able to do more and more each time. It's all right if in the beginning you can only concentrate with fifty or sixty percent of your energy. Gradually, you'll be able to concentrate with the full one hundred percent of your energy. When this happens, then external things will cease to affect you and finally, all that will remain is muji which you are concentrating on with all your being. As you continue to concentrate on just this remaining *muji*, thought after thought, even your doing it will cease to be a problem. And yet, you are still doing it. When this happens, then, although you are doing muji with all your conscious energy, it becomes automatic; and the doing itself becomes a matter of course. In the end, that which is called "I" becomes extremely small, and this objective fact becomes firmly established.

When this happens, "my" effort stops and the effort that intensely plunges deeper and deeper objectively continues. When the subject is completely eliminated, it becomes mindless and selfless. The "I" disappears and "my" voice also completely disappears. Despite the fact that it is mindless and selfless, muji continually springs forth. Muji, which has become purely objectified—the muji of no-thought—becomes the activity of the life of the universe, something entirely pure and untainted. Therefore, since it's an absolute thing, it becomes the cosmic mind or the activity of cosmic life. When this occurs, "I"-consciousness is completely extinguished, and you have completely cut off the thoughts of the small self. At this point, you have reached the state of The Ungraspable.

"Although I have sought this mind, it is ungraspable."

Even though you may feel that this Ungraspable means that you can't get ahold of it, rather, on the contrary, it means that it isn't some thing that cannot be grasped. The state of The Ungraspable springs out of the practice which is practiced through and through. Thus, in this state the "I" is totally dissolved into it, as well as the whole cosmos. This is called "Absolute Mind," or "Cosmic Mind."

When you reach this point, it is the state where you do zazen with heaven and earth filling your *hara.* You should work on muji by placing heaven and earth in your *hara.* When you do this, you will become one with Bodhidharma.

> The Second Patriarch said: Although I have searched
> for this mind, it is utterly ungraspable!

The Second Patriarch Eka Daishi had searched for his mind, but it was completely ungraspable. This means that he had reached the state of Cosmic Mind.

> Bodhidharma said: "Then I have pacified your mind for you."

If you can reach this state, then your mind is truly pacified. All your anxieties and uncertainties are completely blown away and your mind is totally at ease.

When you completely cut yourself off from your individual self, then one becomes zero and zero becomes everything. Since it is such a state, the Second Patriarch Eka and Bodhidharma both intimately illuminate each other; both stand together on the same absolute ground. This is what "only Buddha and Buddha" means. It is the realm of just Buddha and Buddha. So, Bodhidharma said to the Second Patriarch Eka "That's so, that's so."

In any situation it happens in the same way as today's koan, and so we say "face-to-face transmission." Without this intimate meeting of minds, the realm of Oneness can't be grasped. Accordingly, Mumon comments:

> The broken-toothed old barbarian proudly came 100,000 *li* across the sea.

Since Bodhidharma was over one hundred years old when he came to China, some of his teeth had probably fallen out. However, accord-

ing to the usual understanding of Buddhism, the accomplishment of the
Buddha Way required a long process of spiritual development spanning
a number of lives. Against this, Bodhidharma taught, "Seeing into the
nature and becoming Buddha" *(kenshō jōbutsu)*. There is also a legend
which says that members of other sects persecuted Bodhidharma and
stoned him, and so knocked out his teeth. "The toothless old barbarian"
is no other than Bodhidharma, who crossed 100,000 *li* of rough seas
and finally reached China after three years. He came neither to enhance
his own position nor to gain renown, but so that the Buddha-dharma
could be transmitted to China and Japan. In order to express his deep
appreciation, Mumon says: "The broken-toothed old barbarian proudly
came 100,000 *li* across the sea." This doesn't mean that he came for his
own good—rather, from the overflowing of his compassionate heart, he
stirred his old bones and came. His coming to China was like the old
blind Chinese priest Kanjin's coming to Japan.

> It could be said that this was raising waves without any wind.

Although it wasn't necessary for him to come, he came because
his compassionate heart to save all sentient beings overflowed, because
he had an inexhaustible bodhi-mind.

> In the end, he had only one disciple, and even he was a cripple. Alas!

There are many instances in Zen where extremely disparaging words
are used to express praise. Here, Priest Mumon (praises Bodhidharma) by
saying, "In the end, he had only one disciple, and although it was good
to have saved him, he was merely a cripple." Then he says: "Alas"—
this word truly has a profound significance.

> Shasanrō doesn't even know four characters.

Sha is a Chinese surname, and *sanrō* means 'third son'. It indicates
a common person who can't even read the letters inscribed on a coin—
in other words, no learning. What is meant by "no learning" in Zen is

exactly the opposite of what is usually meant by "no learning." As far as Zen study is concerned, that which is to be investigated thoroughly is not objective reality, but one's own matter. It is the investigation of the self. If you thoroughly know yourself, it is not necessary to know anything more; because if you really investigate yourself, there is nothing else. It's something truly marvellous. The investigation of one's own matter is the starting point of Buddhism: the self searches for the self. As the self does this, the self gradually becomes empty; and when this emptiness is thoroughly penetrated, the state where "one is zero" comes about—this zero is wisdom. When the state of zero is reached, then this zero as it is becomes everything. This everything means that one's whole body is the entire cosmos. The study of Buddhism is the study which concentrates on the self. When this self is thoroughly penetrated, the self is no other than the entire cosmos. Going further, when you reach the state where one is everything, the human situation and the origin of the cosmos are at once completely fathomed. Then there's no enlightenment to seek above and there are no sentient beings to save below. Reaching this profound state is what is meant by "no learning." When "no learning" is spoken of in Zen, it is an ideal which means having accomplished what has to be accomplished—or having graduated. Thus, although "Shasanrō doesn't even know four characters" smacks of not knowing anything whatsoever, it means having thoroughly penetrated the deepest principles of learning. Both Bodhidharma and the Second Patriarch Eka have truly attained no learning. The ideal has been completely realized. Mumon thus also praises the disciple's wonderful accomplishment.

Mumon's verse says:

> Coming from the west and directly pointing—
> The affairs are caused by the transmission.

Bodhidharma came from the west and what did he do? He said "That's so, that's so." Without teaching about this and that, he caused his disciples to see directly into their own minds, saying, "Bring me your uneasy mind!" He taught that when the self thoroughly penetrates the real self, then the true self is met. Socrates also taught, "Know yourself." When the Second Patriarch met the true self and realized the state in which the mind is utterly ungraspable, Bodhidharma approved him, saying, "That's so, that's so." That is what "directly pointing" means. Since Master Eka's self had already merged into this state, there was no need for explanation when Bodhidharma said, "That's so."

> The affairs are caused by the transmission.

Since it was passed on just like water poured from one container into another, the matter of disciple succeeding to the Dharma of his master arose.

> The trouble-maker for Zen monasteries
> Is, after all, you.

After that, just as water is poured from one container into another, the Second Patriarch's Dharma was uninterruptedly passed down from the Third Patriarch Sōsan, to the Fourth Patriarch Dōshin, to the Fifth Patriarch Gunin and to the Sixth Patriarch Enō. The Sixth Patriarch's dharma was passed on to Seigen Gyōshi and Nangaku Ejō and then further divided into the Five Houses and Seven Schools. Twenty-four lines of Zen were brought to Japan—that's how developed it became.

"Zen monastery" *(sōrin)* literally means a thicket, it's said that from ancient times, people dwelt in places overgrown with vegetation. "Trouble" means ruckus or clamor. In other words, since koans and such arose in the monasteries, they stirred up controversies. Thus, "It is, after all, you" means that the one responsible for all this hubbub is you, Bodhidharma. Isn't the reason we all have to bother ourselves with troublesome koans and practice rigorous zazen all due to Bodhidharma's coming from the west? Saying so, even though it seems as if Mumon is shaking his finger at Bodhidharma, truly it was just because of Bodhidharma that the spirit of the east—the root of the culture that made it possible for Zen to develop endlessly—was transplanted to China. This is an example of *yokuge no takujō*—the kind of expression where it superficially seems as if Bodhidharma is being put down, but in actuality he is being praised.

CHAPTER 7

"ROSO FACES THE WALL"
The Book of Equanimity, Case 23
Taizan Maezumi Roshi

Preface to the Assembly

Bodhidharma's nine years are known as "wall-gazing." Shinkō's three prostrations are outflowings of heavenly activity. How can the traces be swept away, the footprints be eliminated?

Main Case

Attention! Whenever Roso saw a monk coming, he would face the wall. Hearing of this, Nansen remarked, "I always tell others to receive directly even before the empty kalpa, and to realize even before the Buddha came into the world—but still I haven't found half a man, let alone a man. If he is thus, he will be stuck in the Year of the Donkey."

Appreciatory Verse

Plain water has flavor, subtly transcending the senses.
It precedes forms, though seeming endlessly to exist.
The Way is precious, though seeming massively to be foolish.
Inscribe designs on a jewel and its glory is lost.
A pearl even from an abyss naturally beckons.
Plenty of bracing air purely burnishes off autumn's swelter;
Far away a single tranquil cloud divides sky and water.

Wall Gazing
by
Taizan Maezumi Roshi

ON THE PREFACE TO THE ASSEMBLY

Preface to the Assembly

Bodhidharma's nine years are known as "wall-gazing."
Shinkō's three prostations are outflowings of heavenly activity. How can the traces be swept away, the footprints be eliminated?

Today is already the third day of sesshin. When you sit well, from around the third day, you can sit better and go deeper into samadhi. Before I begin to interpret these lines, I want to say that I don't know how much you can get out of them. But regardless of where each of us stands, or how long we have practiced, I appreciate each one of us equally, including myself.

In the preface, "Bodhidharma's nine years" of wall-gazing are mentioned. How much do we understand Bodhidharma? How much do we appreciate Bodhidharma? Indeed, it's really amazing how much just one person can do. The second line says "Shinkō". Shinkō was the successor of Bodhidharma. He was Chinese. Probably without Shinkō we couldn't have had such a prosperous Zen heritage; nor would such a heritage have been possible without Bodhidharma.

These days, communication has been so well-developed that being in this country, you can get practically anything from anywhere in the world in a few days if you really want to. But fifteen hundred years ago, how was it? This country became independent only two hundred years ago. Even five hundred years ago, it's hard to imagine how this country was—just deserts, coastlines, the plains, the forests, and very few Indians living with lots of animals. One hundred years ago, how was Los Angeles? When we think of this historical development, it fascinates us. Fifteen hundred years ago, what happened?

Bodhidharma spent three years just to come from India to China. These three years ... it strains our imagination to conceive of the difficulties he must have had, and you may not even believe how old he was—over one hundred years old. It is said he was close to one hundred twenty. Almost unbelievable! Prior to coming to China, he expounded the teaching in India for over sixty years. And before those sixty years of work in India, he served his teacher Hannyatara for forty years. Hannyatara was the favorite priest for the king who was Bodhidharma's father. Bodhidharma was the third son, and even as a child he was a brilliant person. Around the age of ten he was already fairly well enlightened. Anyway, it's altogether an unbelievable story. Then his teacher, Venerable Hannyatara died. He told Bodhidharma, "After sixty or seventy years, go to China. Then expound this teaching in the land of China." So Bodhidharma took his teacher's last will, last advice.

In this country people often ask me, "Bodhidharma was sitting nine years facing the wall—did he want to have enlightenment?" Nine years of just wall-gazing. Of course, that refers to Roso facing the wall in the main case—just wall contemplation, nothing else. Then what is the wall? Those of you doing shikan taza: it's supposed to be wall contemplation. What is the wall? Where is the wall? Some of you are working on muji. Those who are, better memorize all the words that Mumon uses in the comment on the first chapter in the *Gateless Gate.* In that comment he uses the phrase "silver mountain, iron wall." If you contemplate muji, you can't think about it. That's what Mumon says in the beginning, you can't think about it. If you think, that's okay, you think. Sooner or later, you get stuck. When you really get stuck, that's the place, the silver mountain, the iron wall. So, how do you remove it? How do you take care of it? How do you release yourself from such an obstacle? In shikan taza you have to face something else. So, what is it? How do you take care of it?

"Bodhidharma's nine years are known as 'wall-gazing'." Bodhidharma said something like this: "Externally, you eliminate relations between yourself and objects. And internally, don't be gasping." *Aegu* literally means (Roshi breathes deeply). That's physically, see. But mentally—the mental condition is more important—or the psychological, or emotional condition, whatever you call it. Don't be gaspy, be peaceful, quiet. Make your mind like a wall. Then enter into the Way. The key is this *shin shoheki*. Make your mind like the wall. Wall-gazing, that's what it is. The wall stands for immovability, solidity. If you're really solid, un-movable, nothing will disturb you. It's not like a piece of stone or rock, even in the first stage, when you stop making contact with external objects. It doesn't mean to be like a dead man."Perceiving everything, yet undisturbed," that's what it means.

A number of you are working on muji. One of you in dokusan ex-pressed, "I really wish to climb up the silver mountain, the iron wall." How do you climb up? How do you crash through? The silver mountain and iron wall themselves are nothing but muji. So it's a very simple principle. Just be so. That's the way to take care of it.

Bodhidharma's wall-gazing is the same thing. Make your mind as the wall, be the wall. Then get into that. That's shikan taza. It is the im-movable state, and yet in that state all activity is taking place. That's what Roso is doing here—expressing himself totally in that state. What he has been expressing can't be described by words. But that's what Nansen is trying to do. They are practically talking about the same thing.

"Shinkō's three prostrations are outflowings of heavenly activity." "Shinkō's three prostrations" has its origin in a story which I think you have heard. Bodhidharma had four Dharma successors. Maybe on one of the very last days of his life, Bodhidharma asked these four, "Tell me, what is your understanding, realization?" Then the four of them ex-pressed their understanding.

The first one was Dōfuku. What he said is something like this: "My understanding, realization, is not to be apart from words, and not to stick to words. And I freely use words."

The second person was the nun Sōji, the daughter of Emperor Wu in the Yang Dynasty. What she said is something like this: "My realiza-tion is something like Ananda's when he saw the Buddhaland. He just glanced at it and never looked back again."

The third person, Dōiku, said: "The four elements—earth, water, fire, wind—not only make up the world, but also the human body, and are originally empty."

Bodhidharma said to the first: "You have gained my skin." To the second: "You have gained my flesh." To the third: "You have gained my bones."

The last was Shinkō, the Second Patriarch, Eka Daishi. He made three bows, and then just stood beside him without saying anything. Bodhidharma then said: "You have gained my marrow."

Dōgen Zenji writes someplace in the *Shōbōgenzō* "Do not think that skin, flesh, bone and marrow are different depths of their understanding. Their understanding is equal." So that's where "Shinkō's three prostrations are outflowings of heavenly activity" comes from. In his silence, and in his three prostrations, the very best activity is expressed effectively. His three prostrations are nothing but the expression of the dharma itself. That's what Banshō means by outflowings of heavenly activity.

"How can the traces be swept away, the footprints be eliminated?" Even though he did all right, isn't there kind of a trace or footprint still left? It is true whether he prostrated himself three times or not. Dharma is all over, anytime, everywhere. That finishes the Preface to the Assembly and brings up the Main Case.

Tomorrow is already the middle of the sesshin. As you know, the last half goes much faster than the first. In this country, as long as you sit as you have been doing, in one way or another this Way will grow. You are responsible, regardless of male or female, monk, nun or layperson. So please, really take it seriously. That's the reason I talked about Bodhidharma and the others in such a way. It might encourage you to practice harder and better. Regardless of how hard we try, we can hardly pay our debts to them.

TEISHO ON THE MAIN CASE

Main Case

Attention! Whenever Roso saw a monk coming, he would face the wall. Hearing of this, Nansen remarked, "I always tell others to receive directly even before the empty kalpa, and to realize even before the Buddha came into the world—but still I haven't found half a man, let alone a man. If he is thus, he will be stuck in the Year of the Donkey."

Today is already the middle day of this sesshin. I think each of you might have been realizing that the atmosphere in the zendo while you are sitting is getting much more subtle; it is settling down. I noticed those who are in charge of the zendo are encouraging your sitting. Especially for those who are working on muji, please don't be hasty. That's no good. Ideally speaking, just sit well. Let it ripen.

This morning while holding dokusan, I had a flash of thought about the difference between koan study and shikan taza. As I mention from time to time, they are the same thing. Of course they are different, different and yet the same. Along with the lines we appreciate today, we will consider this matter, too. At any rate, since we are already in the last part of this sesshin, please—every bit of a second—take good care of it.

"Whenever Roso saw a monk coming, he would face the wall." What was he doing? A case such as this is really good for us to appreciate in as minute detail as possible. Whenever the monk came after him, he did so without even saying a single word. Regardless of what kind of questions the monk asked him, he just turned around and faced the wall. What is he showing? What is he expressing? What do you hear? He is expressing more than words can express. He is expounding the Dharma which cannot be expressed in words. That's shikan taza.

Maybe you have heard or read about various kinds of zazen. In one way or another, every religion has some kind of meditation. Even in Christianity you have meditation. Prayer itself, in a way, is almost like meditation. Hindus meditate, and so do Taoists and maybe even Confucianists from time to time. They call it quiet thinking. In Yasutani Roshi's book you see *bompu* Zen, *gedo* Zen, *shojo* Zen, *daijo* Zen and *saijojo* Zen.[1] The purposes of meditation can be different, such as for health. Health is not an insulting word. Non-Buddhists have meditation, but their purposes are different. Some practice in order to acquire occult powers. That's *gedo* Zen. They practice in order to improve the physical condition, in order to acquire stronger concentration or in order to center themselves and make themselves stronger. I'm not sure if it's appropriate or not, but these could be called

1. For an explanation of the five varieties of zen, c.f. Kapleau, Philip (ed.), The Three Pillars of Zen, Beacon Press, Boston, pp. 41-46.

Hinayana Zen. They're just concerned about their own salvation or liberation. All these meditations or Zen are in one way or another leaky. We say *urojo. Jo* is 'samadhi.' *Uro* means 'there is a leak,' 'there is delusion.'

Then we say *murojo*, 'no leak in the samadhi'. That's the Zen we have been transmitting. That's what Bodhidharma carried from India to China. Then what makes no leak? Wisdom. So, in one way or another we should become aware of that wisdom. Roso and Nansen are brother monks under Master Baso. Here they are expounding the wisdom from two different perspectives, like from the front and the back. Actually, they are doing the same thing.

Roso's facing the wall: It's an outflowing of heavenly activity. He's just showing the visiting monk the very first principle of life. Everything is just as it is—however, whatever, you see.

And Banshō puts *jakugo* on this: "I have met him already." In Japan an important procedure the first time you meet the roshi is to prepare your own incense, then burn it, show your respect and have your first meeting. That's called *shoken*, and we are not doing it here. Banshō says, "*Shokenryo*" (I have met him already). Who is Roso? He is manifesting himself as muji, or whatever you name it. So where do you meet Master Roso? Where and how? As a matter of fact, that's what all of us are doing here. Also, who is he? To realize each one of us without exception is Roso himself—to realize that is called kensho. You have been constantly meeting him, yet somehow there is something in between. That's what Nansen is trying to clarify. Being brother monks, they know each other quite well.

I want to mention another thing. You may have heard it said, "In the Rinzai school they use koans and in the Soto school we don't use koans." This Roso belongs to the same lineage as Rinzai. Actually, he lived prior to Rinzai, but their common lineage stems from Nangaku Ejō, a Dharma successor of the Sixth Patriarch. One of Nangaku Ejō's Dharma successors was Master Baso. And Baso was the teacher of Nansen and Roso.[2] Then see what it says. Whenever whoever comes, he just

---

2. Baso was also the teacher of Hyakujo. Hyakujo was the teacher of Ōbaku. And Ōbaku was the teacher of Rinzai.

turns around without even saying a single word, and sits. That was his way to free the students, the monks. I one hundred percent guarantee no Soto school teacher nowadays does what he did! So it's all up to the individual teacher, and also his training background, and also his wisdom and his awareness as to how to expound the truth. So in general, regarding our practice, we'd better not be partial.

"Hearing of this, Nansen remarked, 'I always tell others to receive directly even before the empty kalpa.'" A kalpa is a measurement of time. Sensei, would you explain how long one kalpa is.

Sensei: There are different definitions, but one is: Take a rock that's ten cubic miles, and once every century an angel flies down and her wings brush against the rock. When the rock wears out, that's one kalpa.

Roshi: Anyway, we can't even imagine how long a kalpa is. There are four kalpas: the kalpa of growth, the kalpa of dwelling, the kalpa of decay, and the empty kalpa. Even before that empty kalpa, you receive. What does that mean? Here the empty kalpa stands for the time before your conscious mind arises. Receive directly. How much is the distance between the empty kalpa and right now?

> I always tell others to receive directly even before the empty kalpa,
> and to realize even before the Buddha came into the world.

After Buddha appeared, people started to worry about delusion and enlightenment. We are deluded. He's enlightened. What's that? Prior to such a dualistic way of dealing with life, immediately grasp what life is.

"—but still I haven't found half a man, let alone a man." These are a kind of figure of speech. It's very difficult to find the person. That is to say, only few can really appreciate.

"If he is thus," and Roso is just doing like that, "He'll be stuck in the Year of the Donkey." There is no such year as the Year of the Donkey! In the Chinese calendar, which we also use in Japan, there is a cycle of twelve different years. First comes the mouse, then ox, tiger, rabbit, dragon, snake, horse, sheep, monkey, cock, dog, and bull. Unfortunately, we don't have the donkey. He is stuck in the Year of the Donkey. So, in other words, regardless of how many years you spend, you'll never come to an end.

So, all those working on breathing, please don't think that

breathing as such is an exercise for beginners. Not at all so, not at all. We can say koan study was in existence since the time of the Buddha. But structured koan study as we know it is a very recent thing. Years ago, all they did was contemplate breathing as perhaps the most common practice. Then they attained awakening through that. But in almost twenty-five hundred years since the Buddha and the thousands of years before that in India, they developed effective means of practice. Each practice has its own unique advantages and disadvantages. But the point is this immovability, as Bodhidharma mentioned. It's not a sticky thing. Make your mind like a huge wall. Nothing, no one, can break through. Then your life becomes undistracted. So please have really good conviction and faith and trust in yourself, in your practice. And with deep devotion and aspiration, just keep on going.

TEISHO ON THE APPRECIATORY VERSE

Appreciatory Verse

Plain water has flavor, subtly transcending the senses.
It precedes forms, though seeming endlessly to exist.
The Way is precious, though seeming massively to be foolish.
Inscribe designs on a jewel and its glory is lost.
A pearl even from an abyss naturally beckons.
Plenty of bracing air purely burnishes off autumn's swelter;
Far away a single tranquil cloud divides sky and water.

Today is already the fifth day, tomorrow is the sixth day, and the next day sesshin will be over. Some of you must have fairly bad pain in your legs. It depends on the individual's bone and muscle structure—mostly the muscle structure and tight tendons. Some have more trouble or pain than others. Regardless of how much pain you have, I want you to sit well. If the pain is too bad, sitting on a chair is quite all right. Our practice is not asceticism. As Dōgen Zenji said, zazen is supposed to be very comfortable and peaceful. So I want you to sit comfortably. But just being comfortable is not enough.

Before getting in too far, I want to review briefly what zazen is. We say *shikan taza*. In that phrase or word, we find 'just sitting'. *Shikan* is 'just' or 'only'. *Ta* means 'just me', practically nothing emphasized. And *za* means 'sitting', 'just sitting'. But the point is to see the content of sitting. It should be sitting. Just physically sitting on the cushion is not sitting. Let the body sit, and also breathing sits, and your mind sits. In a sense, body and mind are not two but one. If you really make your body sit, mind is supposed to sit, too. So when you really make yourself sit, then that's zazen. Just sitting on the cushion, the mind wanders around. That's not zazen.

For convenience, we can sort of think in this way. First we have to physically sit. It's almost like catching a wild horse, tying it to a post. Then, gradually tame it. But it's running around, trying to get out. The first stage, to catch the horse and tie it, is almost like *za*, the sitting part. At the beginning, it's really painful, especially during sesshin. We have to get up early in the morning, sit until nine o'clock or so, all day long. Many of you have been struggling with it, just to sit. So then tame it down. That's the part of *zen.*

We try to calm our busy mind down, and soothe the painful body, get used to it and let the body take it. Originally, the word *zen*, as you know, derived from the Sanskrit term *dhyana*, which means 'quiet thinking'. Instead of letting our conscious mind go wild, think quietly. Let the body calm down first. Then try to let the mind calm down, too. Then in order to do so, as one of the effective means, we use techniques such as breathing. We concentrate on breathing by counting breaths or following breaths. Then try to calm it down.

The next process is to get into samadhi, really focus upon one single thing. Then become one with the object. So if you work on muji, become one with it. If you are counting the breath, become one with the counting. If you do shikan taza, become zazen yourself. By doing so, you get into samadhi. Then, when you really get into samadhi, eventually you forget yourself—dichotomy in one way or another is transcended.

First, what happens is you forget yourself; and technically, that stage is called, "man is forgotten, man empty." And yet there is the object on which you're concentrating. So you go farther into samadhi, then that object is also eliminated. That is called "dharma is empty." Then when that samadhi really ripens, we say, "both man and dharma are empty," and that state is called *Great Death*. That state is sort of the ideal condition of samadhi. But it's static. So remaining in that is no good. You forget about everything, but it's very static, no activity, no function. So it must function. That functioning of samadhi is wisdom. Once you really reach to that Great Death, then *Great Rebirth* will be in realization. So this is the fundamental principle, or process.

Then, the first opening-up or first breaking-through experience takes place along with emptying yourself. Even not completely empty-ing yourself in the ideal way, it happens. But when it's not complete, what you see is also rather limited and partial. That's what happens in many cases. In other words, before samadhi really ripens, you can have that experience. These days, we call that experience kensho. Strictly speaking, until you really come to the point where you eliminate sub-jects and objects altogether, you can't really say that you really attain enlightenment as such. When you realize that, that's what great enlight-enment means. So even for those who have had that breaking-through experience, in that sphere of emptying, practically each individual differs one from the other. The clarity is different. Maybe no two persons are exactly the same, because it is still partial.

What I want to emphasize is sitting itself. In order to get into that samadhi your sitting is supposed to be right. Otherwise, your mind just gets busy and you can't really get into the deep concentration.

When I look at it, some of your postures are much too weak. My posture isn't so good, especially when I talk and hold dokusan. My back is bent, almost like a cat. But it's supposed to be a very well-balanced posture. Again, just making your back straight is not quite enough.

Place the weight of the body in the proper place. The center of gravity of the body is supposed to fall in the center of the triangle formed by the two knees and the base of the spine. In order to do so, shift the gravity of your upper body slightly forward. Try to move al-together, almost like pushing in between your two hip joints. By doing so, the point of that gravity of the upper body is shifted.

When I look at your posture, some of you look rounded in your lower back. It's a very weak position and you can't really have that strength in your lower abdomen. So just making it straight is not enough. Shift it forward. Then don't make too much arch in your lower back. If you do too much, you start having pain. So, having that kind of disposition of the upper body, the center of gravity falls down into the center of that triangle. This is the base for the sitting. Sensei has a crooked back, but even so he can do that. When I hold dokusan, I sit somewhat bent but still try to let the center of gravity fall down. When you sit, when you do zazen, please remember this and try to let your body really sit well.

When you sit like this, you will naturally start feeling slight tension in your lower abdomen, even without putting any artificial effort or strain on it. I want to remind you not to strain. That's what some of you do. Especially those who are working on muji have that tendency. Those concentrating on breathing become too conscious about it and unconsciously tighten up that stomach area trying to breathe deeply. That's very bad. Tightening the muscles around the stomach, the stomach can't function. So avoid that. And if you can't have any strength in the lower abdomen, I would rather advise you don't try pushing hard. Just wait until that strength comes naturally and try to have proper sitting. That's very important.

Another thing is to concentrate in the lower abdomen, the area known as the hara. It's like a centripetal force. Then, when you sit, you can imagine all of the energy of all parts of the body flowing back into that area, and at the same time that energy permeates into all parts of your body, too, so that going to the center and going out from the center, these two energies are balanced. That balanced condition is almost like zero. There is no conflict of any power or energy within the body. Physically, you can balance. Having that center of gravity placed in the lower portion of the abdomen, you are sitting in a very solid state. Then it starts creating, starts generating the energy by itself. That's what we call *jōriki*, 'power of stability'. It's almost physical power. That's what I want you to acquire first.

Sometimes I say when you do sit well, this smoggy, dirty air of Los Angeles becomes tasty. That's true. I'm sure you don't believe it, but

anyway, that's what it says in the appreciatory verse. The first line says, "Plain water has flavor"

We translated plain water. Very plain, but in that plainness there is terrific taste. Water in a way is tasteless, but nobody really says that it's totally tasteless, not at all. Especially when we drink fresh spring water, especially during summer. Climb up the mountain and find the fountain or find the very chill spring. Drink it. What kind of taste does it have? Almost incredible taste. That's what Tendo says here, plain water has flavor.

Of course, this plain state—that's the state of zazen. It is Roso's wall-gazing, Bodhidharma's wall-gazing, and it also refers to your zazen, too. It's plain. Who believes that we sit eight, nine, ten hours a day just doing nothing but sit? People say you're crazy. Right? They like beer or soda or Coca Cola. It's more tasty for them. Like going to the beach or a picnic, it's more tasty. But in this zazen, when you really do it, there is terrific taste.

"Subtly transcending the senses." We translated *joi* as senses. But *joi* is more than that. *Jo* means 'feeling' or 'mind' or 'emotion', and *i* means 'words' or 'verbal expression'. That is what is transcended. In other words, that very subtle taste in zazen; it's indescribable. These lines refer to Roso's zazen.

"It precedes forms, though seeming endlessly to exist." What exists is that subtle taste, subtle zazen. The word we translated as form actually means our conscious mind, our discriminative mind. It says "seeming." By saying so, it gives more of a nuance than if it were just stated. Purposely, Master Tendo expresses it in that way. Thus it expresses the more subtle content of zazen. That's before your discriminative mind functions. That is to say, as long as you are being conscious of your discriminative mind, you can't appreciate this subtlety in zazen. You are just involved with your own talk or ideas. You can't go beyond that. Then you are bound by limited ideas. This subtle flavor precedes form, thought, and ideas. Then it endlessly exists.

"The Way is precious, though seeming massively to be foolish." It's a nice statement. Actually, that "massively" is a description of a high, solid mountain. In *Fukanzazengi* Dōgen Zenji said, "Just like a mountain, sit and get into samadhi, sitting samadhi." Your zazen is supposed to be like a huge immovable mountain, just like a fool. Again, it refers to Master Roso. Whoever comes, he turns around and just sits, just like a fool. Seems like an idiot, like a fool, but he's not, and he's not a holy man either. He doesn't fall into enlightenment or delusion, good, bad, right or wrong. He transcends all these dichotomies, and expresses the Dharma as is. That's what it says, "the Way is precious." No way is better than that.

"Inscribe designs on a jewel and its glory is lost." The jewel again— you do zazen. Here, it particularly refers to Roso's wall-gazing. And what is the inscription? It's Nansen's remark. In a way, it is true. When you really get into deep samadhi, then open up the eye of wisdom and just sit. What else besides that is necessary to describe? Everything is there—but Nansen telling the people you have to receive it directly even prior to the empty kalpa is almost a joke. We don't need that kind of comment. Koans are similar to that. Not studying koans would be one hundred percent okay. By doing that kind of thing, in a way we defile the genuineness of our life, of our being. "Inscribe designs on a jewel and its glory is lost." It s very best part is somewhat missed.

"A pearl even from an abyss naturally beckons." Again, he is praising Roso's genuine zazen. Even though he doesn't say a word, that jewel, pearl, shines as is.

"Plenty of bracing air purely burnishes off autumn's swelter. Far away a single tranquil cloud divides sky and water." Again, these two lines refer to Roso's wall-gazing. It's like bracing air in early autumn, so refreshing. That genuine zazen cools off our hot heads. "Far away a single tranquil cloud divides sky and water." It almost refers to Nansen's position, commenting on his words. It's almost as if he's dividing something else, like air from earth, sky from water. And yet what he is himself is like a single piece of cloud crossing the sky, according to the wind. It doesn't matter where it flies. With nothing sticking to it, and leaving no trace, no footprint, it just goes wherever it's supposed to. "Plenty of bracing air purely burnishes off autumn's swelter. Far away a single tranquil cloud divides sky and water."

So sesshin is almost over. All the last part goes fast. That means we can sit better. Please, try to have a good sesshin.

THE SIXTEEN PRECEPTS

The Three Treasures

Be one with the Buddha
Be one with the Dharma
Be one with the Sangha

The Three Pure Precepts

Do not commit evil
Do good
Do good for others

The Ten Grave Precepts

Do not kill
Do not steal
Do not be greedy
Do not tell a lie
Do not be ignorant
Do not talk about others' faults
Do not elevate yourself by criticising others
Do not be stingy
Do not get angry
Do not speak ill of the Three Treasures

BODHISATTVA'S PRECEPTS AND
THE CAPACITY FOR BODHISATTVA'S PRECEPTS
Selection from Jiun Sonja Hōgoshū
Translated by Taizan Maezumi Roshi
with John Daishin Buksbazen

Jiun Sonja (1718-1804) was the founder of the Vinaya subsect of Shingon Buddhism. He also studied Zen under Soto Master Daibai at Shoanji Temple in Shin-Shu province. He was an outstanding Sanskrit scholar and was also well-versed in Confucianism, Shinto and other fields of learning and literature. As an artist, he is especially well-known for his dry-brush style of calligraphy. This selection is from the book *Jiun Sonja Hōgoshū* (A Collection of Jiun Sonja's Dharma Words), published by Sanmitsudo, Kyoto, 1971.

Bodhisattva's Precepts and the Capacity for Bodhisattva's Precepts

The precepts are the precepts in one's own mind. That is to say, [they are] the precepts of Buddha-nature. Samadhi and wisdom are the same samadhi and wisdom within one's mind. That is to say, [they are] the samadhi and wisdom of Buddha-nature.

Only the Buddha, the World-honored One, has attained supreme enlightenment. Seeing that the Precepts-dharma is already inherent in the minds of all sentient beings, he expounded upon it. That is the Precepts-dharma which I will give you. Realizing this samadhi and wisdom originally in the mind of each sentient being, that is the sutras.

As for the capacity of sentient beings, this Precepts-dharma can be described as great or small. If you receive this Precepts-dharma, still being attached to the body and mind of the Five Skandhas, and wishing to liberate this body and mind, all the precepts you receive will become the Sravaka Precepts.

If there is a man who understands that from the beginning the Form-dharma of the Five Skandhas is like a cloud in the sky and that the Mind-dharma is like the reflection of the moon in the water, and realizing that all sentient beings and oneself are originally equal and can be said neither to be one or many; and raising the Great Four Vows to receive these precepts, then the precepts you receive become the Bodhisattva's Precepts.

Due to receiving the precepts while attached to body and mind, the very body of the precepts will decline in accord with the destruction of body and mind.

While the Bodhisattva's Precepts are apart from attachment to the Five Skandhas, and [one] receives them with equal and vast mind, the precepts-body flows into the ocean of the future kalpa.

Buddha expounded the Five Different Natures in the sutra. Although he talks about Five Natures, they are one Dharma-nature. Although it is one Dharma-nature, it doesn't hurt at all to talk about it as Five Natures.

In these days, people are attached to worldly fame and profit, being greedy and filled with the Five Desires and unable to raise aspiration toward the right Dharma for even a short while. Being attached on top of attachment, and being greedy on top of greed, moreover, raising all sorts of worldly cleverness, sophistry, deluded views, and evil states of mind, they embellish their errors and accumulate misdeeds without realizing their own shamefulness. Occasionally they have a chance to hear the right Dharma and to see the Buddha's sutras, but they do not raise the faith. People of this sort are called "Animate beings of no nature." It could be said that temporarily [their] Buddha-nature has disappeared.

These days there are many people of this kind in the world. Even if perchance they have had jukai, still this amounts to only a tenuous [karmic] connection. Indeed, such a person does not have the capacity for the Bodhisattva's Precepts.

Again, there is a group of sentient beings who, realizing the impermanence of worldly desires and knowing the awfulness of life and death, and who, understanding the necessity of practicing the precepts, samadhi, and wisdom, willingly seek for the Dharma of tranquil Nirvana. If we compare these people to the previous group, there is the difference between Heaven and Earth; and yet, due to not raising that vast mind, not realizing that they're originally equal to all sentient beings, and just wanting partial liberation for themselves; this too is not the capacity for the Bodhisattva's Precepts. This is called the Sravaka-seed Nature.

Again, among these, some brilliant individuals, without waiting for others to expound the Dharma, practice and enlighten [themselves], profoundly contemplating on the karmic causations of birth and death, by themselves. These people are superior to the former group, and yet due to not raising the true Bodhi-mind, being attached to one's own mind, this is also not the capacity for the Bodhisattva's Precepts. This is called Pratyeka-seed Nature.

Again, if there is a person who realizes that the body and mind of the Five Skandhas are like a cloud in the sky, like the moon in the water, and that all beings and their lands in the Ten Spheres are nothing but the manifestation of one's own mind, and who raises the equal, unconditioned, compassionate mind toward all sentient beings, all of whose deeds are dedicated to the animate beings in the Dharma-worlds, and who offers his own life in order to seek the Supreme Way; this kind of person is one who has the true [right] capacity to receive the Bodhisattva's Precepts. Contemplating and considering like this, with sincere devoted heart [mind], receive the Dharma of the Precepts.

—opening remarks at Jukai, Bosatsukai Dōjō
November 11, 1761

EXAMPLES OF KOANS: TEN CASES FROM
THE BOOK OF EQUANIMITY (SHŌYŌ ROKU CASES 46-55)

Translated by Taizan Maezumi Roshi and Dana Fraser

The Book of Equanimity consists of one hundred cases. Each case consists of an old koan accompanied by an introductory preface and an appreciatory verse. The koans were originally selected and compiled by the Sung Dynasty Soto Zen Master Tendo Wanshi Shogaku (1091-1157) in twelfth century China. He also added his appreciatory verse to each koan, following the example of Master Setchō Juken (980-1052), the compiler of *The Blue Cliff Records.* The preface to each case was added at a later time by another Soto teacher, Master Banshō Gyōshū (1166-1246). He gave a series of talks to his disciples on the original koans and Master Tendo's verses. Master Banshō also made *jakugo* or capping phrases for each main case and appreciatory verse and added a long commentary to each case. The capping phrases and commentary are not translated here, but are sometimes mentioned by Maezumi Roshi in his teisho.

These koans and the accompanying verses have been abstracted from their culture and time period. The limited notes appended here are not intended to explain all the historical or cultural references which may be unfamiliar to the general reader. The cases are presented as a collection of certain Zen principles and subtle degrees of understanding, valid for every human now and in the future. Where the Chinese characters are deliberately ambiguous, as when the subject and/or object of a verb has been omitted, the English should preserve that ambiguity. In cases where conventional words or grammar fail to meet the need, we improvise in some way to match the meaning of the original. If the English meaning or punctuation seems odd on first reading, it often becomes clear if the reader simply continues on and comes back to it later. If the result is still not clear to the reader (and assuming our English is accurate), the reader then knows that the mental state or principal point illustrated by it may not have been personally experienced by him and therefore cannot be understood yet. Every koan may be regarded by the reader as one part of a rigorous comprehensive examination in Zen Buddhist study. Even when a clear intuitive understanding of a koan has been reached, the student may still be required by his teacher to present a *jakugo* or capping phrase to sum up his understanding intellectually. People respond to the same koan in different ways, and each person will find some more difficult than others.

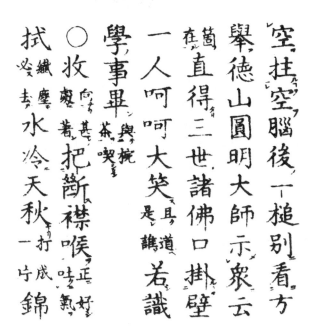

Shōyō Rōku, Case 46; part of the Introduction, Main Case
and Appreciatory Verse, with Capping Phrases

The *Shōyō roku* is currently being published in English for the first time by the Zen Center of Los Angeles. The translations of the cases into English by Maezumi Roshi and Dana Fraser are the most complete of any so far.

CASE 46: TOKUSAN'S COMPLETION OF STUDY

Preface to the Assembly

The pure ground [even] without ten thousand *li* or an inch of grass still deludes men. The clear sky even without a speck of cloud deceives you. Though wedges are driven in and pulled out, this does not impede the holding up and supporting of space. A hammer blow on the back of the head—let's look at a skillful expedient.

Main Case

Attention! Great Teacher Emmyō Tokusan addressed the assembly, saying, "Exhaust the end and there's instant attainment: the mouths of all Buddhas of the three times [might as well] hang upon a wall. Now, there's a man who roars with laughter, Ha! Ha! When you know him, the essence of your exhaustive study is completed."

Appreciatory Verse

> Gathering.
> Seizing the throat collar.
> Winds burnish, clouds sweep;
> Chilling water, heaven turns to autumn.
> Don't say the silken scale[1] lacks taste;
> Catching all with Sōrō's crescent moon.[2]

---

1. Here means fish scale.
2. Here Sōrō means the vast ocean. Cf. Case 12.

CASE 47: JŌSHŪ'S CYPRESS TREE

Preface to the Assembly

The cypress tree in the garden, the flapping flag on the pole. As a blossom bespeaks the boundless spring, a drop bespeaks the ocean's water. The five-hundred-year-old buddha clearly leaves the usual stream. Not falling into speech or thought how do you express it!

Main Case

Attention! A monk asked Jōshū, "What is the meaning of Bodhidharma's coming from the West?"

Jōshū answered, "The cypress tree in the garden."

Appreciatory Verse

Eyebrow-banks snow tipped, river-eyes embracing autumn;
Ocean-mouth booming out waves, sail-tongue drifting downstream.
Riot-quelling hand, peace-making strategy—
Dear old Jōshū, dear old Jōshū!
Stirring up the monastery, he's not yet taken rest;
Uselessly rendering aid, making a cart and entering ruts;
Basically untalented, blocking up ravines and filling ditches.

CASE 48: THE VIMALAKIRTI SUTRA'S "NOT TWO"

Preface to the Assembly

Marvelous activity may be limitless, but there is a place where the hand cannot reach; speech may be unimpeded, but there's a time when the mouth can't be open. As Ryūge was a handless man who used his fist, so Kassan the tongue-less man used words to cause understanding.[1] To liberate the body when halfway down the road—who is such a man!

Main Case

Attention! Vimalakīrti asked Manjusri, "What about a bodhisattva entering the non-dual Dharma-gate?"

Manjusri replied, "As I understand it, with regard to all dharmas there are no words or speech, no revelation or knowledge, and it is separate from all conversation. This is entering the non-dual Dharma-gate."

Thereupon Manjusri questioned Vimalakīrti, saying, "All of us [bodhisattvas] have each had our say. Venerable sir, now you should expound about a bodhisattva entering the non-dual Dharma-gate."

Vimalakīrti maintained silence.

Appreciatory Verse

Manjusri's sick-call to old Vaisali.[2]
The non-dual gate opens—look at the adept.
Rough outside, genuine within—who appreciates him!
Forgetting "before" and losing "after," don't lament.
Trying hard to offer a stone[3]—the offender at So's palace.
In recompense the luminous jewel—the wounded snake at Zui's castle.
Stop inquiring—it's beyond flaws;
Totally lacking worldliness—that's worth a little.

---

1. Cf. Case 36, Main case.
2. The town in India where it is said Vimalakīrti lived.
3. Cf. Case 2.

CASE 49: TŌZAN OFFERS TO THE ESSENCE

Preface to the Assembly

Sketching it doesn't succeed, and coloring it doesn't. Fuke thereupon turned a somersault; Ryūge revealed only half his body. In the end, what are the features of *that* man?

Main Case

Attention! When Tōzan was conducting a memorial service to Ungan's essence, he related the story of how [Ungan was once asked by him] to reveal his essence. A monk who was present asked, "What did Ungan intend by saying, 'Just *this*'?"

Tōzan replied, "At that time I almost completely misunderstood my late teacher's intent."

The monk asked, "Did Ungan know [of 'just *this*'] ?"

Tōzan replied, "If he didn't know, how could he speak thus; if he did know, why did he even speak thus."

Appreciatory Verse

How could he speak thus;
Fifth watch, and a cock crows dawn in the forest of houses.
Why did he even speak thus;
Thousand year old crane and cloud-piercing pine together grow old.
The jewelled mirror lucidly tests absolute and relative;
The bejewelled loom with shuttle flying—see the unstopped finish.
The School's style prospering greatly—rules mosey along;
Father and son transforming throughout—voice-charisma expanding.

CASE 50: SEPPŌ'S "WHAT'S THIS!"

Preface to the Assembly

The last word ultimately reaches the dense barrier. Being proud, Gantō above did not approve his closest teacher, and below did not concede anything to his Dharma brother [Seppō].[1] Is this a trying to create an echelon, or is there some other vital function?

Main Case

Attention! When Seppō was dwelling in a hut, two monks came and both made a prostration. Seppō, having seen them come, threw open the hut door, burst outside, and shouted "What's this!"

One monk repeated, "What's this!"

Seppō hung his head and went back inside the hut.

The monk later arrived at Gantō's place. Gantō asked, "Where have you come from?"

The monk replied, "Reinan [province]."

Gantō asked, "Did you ever visit Seppō?"

The monk answered, "Yes, I did."

Gantō asked, "Did he have anything to say?" The monk related the previous incident.

Gantō asked, "Was there anything else?"

The monk replied, "He said nothing, but hung his head and went back in the hut."

Gantō remarked, "Ahh, I should have told him the last word that one time. If I had told him, no man under heaven could do anything with him."

At the end of the summer session, the monk repeated the previous story and asked for some guidance. Gantō said, "Why didn't you ask sooner!"

The monk replied, "It's not an easy thing to ask."

Gantō remarked, "We were born of the same branch, but we will not die of the same branch. If you would know the last word, it is 'just this'!"

Appreciatory Verse

> Cutting, polishing, transforming, and veiling.
> Kappi [pond's] dragon-transformed stick;[2]
> Tōka's wall-hung shuttle.[3]
> Many born of the same branch, but
> Few who die of the same branch.
> The last word is, "just this;"
> A wind-boat, having loaded the moon, bobs on autumn waters.

---

1. See Cases 22 and 55.
2. This refers to a story about a man who went to a hermit's place, tried to learn the man's magical powers, and finally gave up and wanted to go home. The hermit gave him a bamboo stick to fly home with, and told him to throw the stick into Kappi pond after he arrived. He did, and the stick changed into a dragon who flew back to the hermit.
3. This refers to a legend about a boy named Tokan who netted a shuttle from a loom while fishing. Thinking it unusual, he took it home and hung it on the wall. Later, during a thunderstorm, the shuttle turned into a dragon and flew away. Just as this couplet refers to an ordinary object changed into a superior being, so Gantō tried to make the monk an enlightened man.

CASE 51: HŌGEN'S "BY BOAT OR LAND?"

Preface to the Assembly

Worldly dharmas enlighten many people; Buddha dharma deludes many people. Suddenly become one, and can there be any delusion or enlightenment!

Main Case

Attention! Hogen asked Kaku *jōza*, "Coming by boat or by land?"
Kaku replied, "Coming by boat."
Hōgen asked, "Where is the boat?"
Kaku answered, "The boat is in the river."
After Kaku left, Hōgen asked the monk beside him, "Tell me, did that monk who was just here have the Zen eye or not?"

Appreciatory Verse

> Water doesn't wash water,
> Gold doesn't trade for gold.
> Ignoring its color, obtain a horse;
> Without its strings, enjoy a lute.
> Tying a knot, divining with sticks,
>   there is this matter—
> Utterly lost is true, innocent, ancient mind.

CASE 52: SŌZAN'S DHARMAKAYA

Preface to the Assembly

All knowledgeable men are able to learn by parable and analogy. When comparison cannot be made, and when it's impossible to find something similar or identical, how can it be expressed!

Main Case

Attention! Sōzan asked Toku *jōza*, "Buddha's true Dharmakaya is like the vast sky. Its conforming to things and manifesting shapes is like the moon in water. How can this principle of conforming be expressed?"
    Toku said, "It's like a donkey seeing a well."
    Sōzan remarked, "Well said, but that's only eighty percent of it."
    Kaku rejoined, "How about you, Oshō?"
    Sōzan replied, "The well sees the donkey."

Appreciatory Verse

> Donkey sees well; well sees donkey.
> Wisdom contains without exception.
> Purity permeates more than enough.
> Behind the elbow, who discerns the sign;
> Within the house, no books are kept.
> Loom threads don't hang—a matter of the shuttle;
> Patterns every which way—the intent of itself differentiates.

CASE 53: ŌBAKU'S DREGS

Preface to the Assembly

Having an opportunity and not seeing a buddha. Great enlightenment has no teacher. Human emotions are eliminated by the sword that regulates heaven and earth; holy understanding is forgotten in the activity that catches tigers and buffalos. Tell me, whose stratagem is this?

Main Case

Attention! Ōbaku addressed the assembly, saying, "All of you without exception are wine-dreg-eating fellows. Pilgrimaging thus, when will there ever be a day for you? Don't you know there are no Zen masters in all of T'ang China?"

At that time a monk who was there stepped forward and said, "But what about those everywhere who have disciples and lead assemblies?"

Ōbaku remarked, "I don't say there is no Zen, just that there are no teachers."

Appreciatory Verse

> Roads being split, threads being dyed—how bothersome!
> Catching at leaves and lining up flowers ruins the Patriarchs.
> Subtly grasping the handle that educates Southerners;
> The water-and-cloud [-inscribing] tool's with the potter's wheel.
> Tangles and shards removed and crushed, downy hairs razored off.
> Balance scale, bright mirror, jewelled ruler, golden sword—
> Old Ōbaku [even] divines autumn fur,[1]
> Cutting off the spring breeze, not allowing hauteur.

---

1. In autumn the fur of a rabbit is said to become subtly finer.

CASE 54: UNGAN'S GREAT COMPASSIONATE ONE

Preface to the Assembly

The eight compass points bright and clear, the ten directions unobstructed. Everywhere bright light shakes the earth. All the time there is marvelous functioning and the supernatural. Tell me, how can this occur!

Main Case

Attention! Ungan asked Dōgo, "What does the Great Compassionate Bodhisattva do when he uses his manifold hands and eyes?"

Dōgo replied, "It's like a man who reaches behind him at night to search for his pillow."

Ungan said, "I understand."

Dōgo asked, "What do you understand?"

Ungan said, "All over the body are hands and eyes."

Dōgo remarked, "You really said it—you got eighty percent of it."

Ungan asked, "Elder brother, how about you?"

Dōgo replied, "Throughout the body are hands and eyes."

Appreciatory Verse

One hole penetrates space; the eight directions are clear and bright.
Without forms, without self, spring follows the rules.
Unstopped, unhindered the moon traverses the sky.
Clean, pure jewelled eyes and virtuous arms.
Where's the approval in "throughout the body" instead of "all over the body?"
The hands and eyes before you manifest complete functioning.
The great function's everywhere—how could there be any hindrance!

CASE 55: SEPPŌ'S COOK

Preface to the Assembly

Ice is colder than water; green comes from blue. When one's viewpoint excels that of the teacher, one is ready for the transmission. If the children who are raised are not equal to their fathers the family will decline in a single generation. Tell me, who is the one who snatches up the father's function?"

Main Case

Attention! Seppō served as cook while at Tokusan's place. One day the meal was late. Tokusan arrived at the Dharma hall holding his bowls. Seppō remarked, "Old fellow, the gong hasn't yet rung, the drum hasn't yet sounded, so where are you going with the bowls?" At that, Tokusan returned to his quarters. Seppō told Gantō about this.

Gantō remarked, "As you might expect, Tokusan doesn't understand the last word yet."

Hearing of this, Tokusan called an attendant and had him go and bring Gantō, and then asked, "Don't you approve this old monk?" Gantō whispered his intended meaning. Thereupon Tokusan desisted.

As you might expect, the next day when he went to the Hall he was not the same as usual. Rubbing his hands and laughing, Gantō cried, "Luckily the old fellow has understood the last word. From now on no one under heaven will be able to do anything with him."

Appreciatory Verse

> The last word—understood or not?
> Tokusan—father and sons—are exceedingly abstruse.
> Within the group there's a guest from Kōnan;
> Don't sing the partridge's song before men.[1]

---

1. Kōnan is a province in southern China noted for its partridges, whose song is said to make men feel nostalgic.

GLOSSARY

An asterisk (*) indicates a foreign word italicized in the Zen Writings Series. Those words of foreign origin without asterisks (unitalicized in the text) are considered to be in relatively common usage in American Zen practice.

ango (lit. "peaceful dwelling"): A practice period, usually three months in length, devoted to meditation, study, and communal work.
*Anuttara Samyak Sambodhi (Skt): Supreme, Complete Awakening.

bodhi-mind (Skt: bodhi-citta; J: bodaishin): The mind of one in whom the desire for enlightenment has been awakened.
bodhisattva (Skt; J: bosatsu): An enlightened being who dedicates himself to helping others become enlightened.
bosatsukai (J) (lit. "a meeting of bodhisattvas"): Can be used to denote any group of Zen Buddhists who meet together for practice.
Buddha-nature: The intrinsic nature of all sentient beings, whether or not realized.
*buji Zen (J) (lit. "no-matter" Zen): An excessively casual attitude toward Zen discipline and training, based on the rationalization that since we are all fundamentally buddhas, we need not bother with practice, morality or realization.

dharma (Skt): Any thing or event.
Dharma (Skt): The teachings of the Buddha; Truth; Buddhist doctrine; universal law.
Dharma brothers: Two or more people who have received Dharma transmission from the same teacher. (See Inka, Shiho.)
Dharma hall: A room or building in a monastery in which the abbot gives his talks on the Dharma; also combined in most places with the Buddha hall, in which services are held.
Dharma name: The name given to someone when he or she receives precepts (jukai), thus formally becoming a Buddhist.
Dharma successor: A person designated by a Zen master to carry on his teaching lineage and authorized to hold dokusan, verify enlightenment experiences, and in turn name Dharma successors.
Dharmakaya (Skt; J: hosshin): One of the three aspects (trikaya) of the Buddha, it is the phenomenal world, in which all things are One.
*dhyana (Skt): Meditation.
*dōjō (J): A training center.

119

dokusan (J): A one-to-one encounter between Zen student and Zen master in which the student's understanding is probed and stimulated and in which the student may consult the teacher on any matters arising directly out of practice.

enlightenment: Realization of one's true nature.

Five Desires: Money or wealth (zai), material things, including sex (shiki), food (jiki), fame (myo), and sleep (sui).

Four Great Vows: "Sentient beings are numberless; I vow to save them. Desires are inexhaustible; I vow to put an end to them. The Dharmas are boundless; I vow to master them. The Buddha-way is unsurpassable; I vow to attain it." Zen students chant these vows daily as an expression of their aspirations.

Fukanzazengi (J) (lit. "Universal Promotion of the Principles of Zazen"): A brief work on how and why to sit zazen, by Dōgen Zenji.

*gakki (J): Memorial service.

Hakuin Ekaku Zenji (1686-1769): The patriarch of Japanese Rinzai Zen, through whom all present-day Rinzai masters trace their lineage. He systematized koan study as we know it today.

*hara (J): The area of the lower abdomen which is the physical center of gravity of the human body, and which becomes a center of awareness in zazen.

*jakugo (J) (lit. "capping phrase"): A pithy expression which concisely summarizes or comments upon part or all of a koan. Zen students who work with koans are traditionally required to find jakugo as part of their koan practice, as further evidence of their understanding.

*jōriki (J) (lit. "samadhi power"): The vital, stabilizing energy arising from strong zazen practice.

jukai (J): Ceremony of receiving the precepts. A person receiving the precepts formally becomes a Buddhist and is given a Dharma name.

*kalpa (Skt): An eon; an extremely long period of time.

Kannon (J; variants: Kanzeon; Kanjizai) (Skt: Avalokitesvara): One of the three principal bodhisattvas in the Zen Buddhist tradition, Kannon is the personification of Great Compassion, and is usually represented in the female form.

karma (Skt): The principle of causality, which holds that for every effect there is a cause, and, in the human sphere, maintains that by our actions we determine the quality of our lives, and influence the lives of others.

Keizan Jōkin Zenji (1268-1325): Fourth patriarch and co-founder, with his predecessor Dōgen Zenji, of the Soto School in Japan, Keizan Zenji was largely responsible for the spread of Japanese Soto Zen, and was particularly noted for his meticulous instructions and procedures governing virtually every aspect of monastic life.

kensho (J) (lit. "seeing into one's own nature"): An experience of enlightenment; also known as satori.

kinhin (J): Walking zazen, usually done for five to ten minutes between periods of sitting zazen.

koan (J): A brief anecdote recording an exchange between master and student, or a master's enlightenment experience. Koans are used in Zen to bring a student to realization, and to help clarify his enlightenment.

kyosaku (J) (lit. "waking stick"): A long stick, generally flattened at one end, the kyosaku is carried in the meditation hall by one or more monitors, who periodically whack sitters on the shoulders to encourage them or to help them stay awake.

*li (Ch): In olden China, about one-third of a mile.

Manjusri (Skt; J: Monju): The Bodhisattva of Wisdom, often depicted riding a lion, holding the sword of wisdom which cuts through delusion. Especially appreciated in the Zen sect, Manjusri Bodhisattva is the principal figure on the zendo altar. *Cf.* Kannon, Samantabhadra.

mu-ji (J): The character "mu", a negative particle used to point directly at reality and which has no discursive content. The use of the word in this sense originated with Master Jōshū Jushin (Ch: Chao-chou, 778-897) who, when asked by a monk, "Does a dog have Buddha-nature?" directly answered, "Mu!" The incident is used as the first koan in *The Gateless Gate (Mumonkan)*.

nirvana (Skt; J: nehan): In Zen practice, a non-dualistic state, beyond life and death.

*oryoki (J) (lit. "that which holds just enough"): Broadly speaking, the nested set of bowls given every monk and nun at ordination, from which meals are eaten. Strictly speaking, the term refers exclusively to the largest of these bowls. In early Buddhist tradition, this bowl was used to collect offerings when the monk or nun would go begging in the street. Nowadays, oryoki are also used by laypersons.

Patriarchs: Strictly speaking, the first thirty-four Dharma successors from Shakyamuni Buddha through the Sixth Chinese Patriarch, Daikan Enō (Ch: Hui-neng,
638-713). More generally, an honorific term used to describe any Zen master
of outstanding attainment.
prajna (Skt; J: hannya): The wisdom of enlightenment.
precepts (Skt: sila; J: kai): Teachings regarding personal conduct, which can be appreciated on a fairly literal level as ethical guidelines, and more broadly as
various aspects or qualities of reality.

Rinzai School: The Zen lineage founded by Master Rinzai Gigen (Ch: Lin-ch'i, d.
866).
roshi (J) (lit. "venerable teacher"): A Zen master.

samadhi (Skt; J: zammai): A state of mind characterized by one-pointedness of attention; in Zen, a non-dualistic state of awareness.
Samantabhadra Bodhisattva (Skt; J: Fugen Bosatsu): One of the three principal
bodhisattvas in the Zen Buddhist tradition, Samantabhadra is associated with
practice and active love. *Cf.* Kannon, Manjusri.
*sambō (J) (lit. "Three Treasures"): 1) A lacquered tray on a pedestal used to make
offerings in Buddhist services. 2) The Three Treasures.
*samu (J): Working zazen, often physical labor, in- or out-of-doors.
Sangha (Skt): Originally, the body of Buddhist monks and nuns, the term "Sangha"
later came to include laypersons as well; in Zen, the harmonious interrelationship of all beings, phenomena, and events.
sesshin (J) (lit. "to collect or regulate the mind"): A number of days set aside for a
Zen meditation retreat.
Shakyamuni (Skt) (lit. "the silent sage of the Shakya clan): The title accorded
Siddartha Gautama upon his becoming the Buddha (i.e., upon his enlightenment).
shikan-taza (J) (lit. "just sitting"): Zazen itself, without supportive devices such as
breath-counting or koan study. Characterized by intense, non-discursive
awareness, shikan-taza is "zazen doing zazen for the sake of zazen".
Shōbōgenzō (J) (lit. *"A Treasury of the Eye of the True Dharma"):* Masterwork of
Dōgen Zenji, founder of the Japanese Soto School of Zen, it comprises some
ninety-five articles dealing with a wide variety of Buddhist topics, and is
generally considered to be one of the most subtle and profound works in
Buddhist literature.
*shōsan (J): A formal meeting in Zen monasteries and centers in which a teacher or
senior student gives a short talk and then engages in question/answer dialogue

with any who wish to challenge his understanding, ask a question, or make a comment. A kind of public dokusan.

*skandhas (Skt) (lit. "heaps, aggregates"): In Buddhist psychology, the five modes of being which, taken collectively, give rise to the illusion of self. They are: form; feeling; thought; discrimination; and perception.

Soto School: The Zen lineage founded by Masters Tōzan Ryokai (Ch: Tung-shan, 807-869), and Sōzan Honjaku (Ch: Ts'ao-shan, 840-901). The Japanese branch of this school was founded by Masters Eihei Dōgen (1200-1254) and Keizan Jōkin (1268-1325).

*sunyata (Skt): Emptiness; the ground of being.

sutras (Skt): Buddhist scriptures; the dialogues and sermons of the Buddha and certain other major Buddhist figures.

*tantō (J): Assistant to the godo; the person in charge of the operations of a zendo.

Tathāgatha (Skt; J: Nyorai): The name the Buddha used in referring to himself, it literally means "thus-come", indicating the enlightened state.

teisho (J): A formal commentary by a Zen master on a koan or other Zen text. In its strictest sense, teisho should be non-dualistic and is thus distinguished from Dharma talks, which are ordinary lectures on Buddhist topics.

Ten Spheres: The realms of buddhas, bodhisattvas, pratyeka-buddhas, sravaka-buddhas, heavenly beings, human beings, fighting spirits, animals, hungry ghosts, and hell-dwellers.

*tenzō (J): Person in charge of the kitchen in a monastery or Zen center. Traditionally, the position of tenzō is considered to be one of the most challenging assignments.

tokudo (J): Ceremony of receiving the precepts. There are two kinds of tokudo: *zaike* tokudo, in which one formally becomes a lay Buddhist; and *shukke* tokudo, in which one becomes a monk or nun.

*vinaya (Skt) (lit. "discipline"): The Buddhist school which most strongly emphasizes monastic discipline as the basis of its practice; generally, the code of conduct upon which this discipline is based.

zazen (J): The practice of Zen meditation.

zendo (J): A place set aside for the practice of Zen.

Zenji (J) (lit. "Zen master"): An honorofic term used to refer to a master of high rank or attainment.

BIBLIOGRAPHY

INTRODUCTORY BOOKS ON ZEN

Herrigel, Eugen. *Zen.* New York: McGraw Hill, 1964. Paperback.
Suzuki, D.T. *An Introduction to Zen Buddhism.* New York: Grove Press, 1964. Paperback.
Watts, Alan W. *The Way of Zen.* New York: Random House, Vintage Books, 1957. Paperback.

PRACTICE-ORIENTED BOOKS ON ZEN

Buksbazen, John Daishin. *To Forget the Self: An Illustrated Introduction to Zen Practice.* Introduction by Hakuyu Taizan Maezumi. Los Angeles: Zen Center of Los Angeles, 1977. Paperback.
Chang, Garma C.C. *The Practice of Zen.* New York: Harper and Row, Perennial Library, 1969. Paperback and hardcover.
Kapleau, Philip, ed. *The Three Pillars of Zen.* Boston: Beacon Press, 1965. Paperback and hardcover.
Suzuki, Shunryu. *Zen Mind, Beginner's Mind.* Edited by Trudy Dixon. New York and Tokyo: John Weatherhill, 1970. Paperback and hardcover.

BOOKS ON THE TRAINING OF ZEN MONKS

Zen Buddhism. Japan Times Photo Book. Tokyo: Japan Times, 1970.
Mishimura, Eshin. *Unsui: A Diary of Zen Monastic Life.* Drawings by Giei Sato. Edited with an introduction by Bardwell L. Smith. Honolulu: University of Hawaii, East-West Center Books, 1973. Paperback.
Sato, Koji. *The Zen Life.* Photographs by Sosei Kuzunishi. Translated by Ryojun Victoria. Tokyo: John Weatherhill, 1972.
Schierbeek, Bert. *Zazen.* Photographs by Else Madelon Hooykaas. Translated by Charles McGeehan. Tucson, Ariz.: Omen Press, 1974. Paperback.
Suzuki, D.T. *The Training of the Zen Buddhist Monk.* Illustrated by Zenchu Soto. Berkeley: Wingbow Press. Paperback.

BOOKS ON KOANS, BY ZEN MASTERS

Miura, Isshu, and Ruth Fuller Sasaki. *The Zen Koan.* New York: Harcourt, Brace and World, 1965. Paperback and hardcover.

Shibayama, Zenkei. *Zen Comments on the Mumonkan.* Translated by Sumiko Kudo. New York: Mentor, 1974. Paperback and hardcover.

WORKS OF CONTEMPORARY MASTERS

Hasegawa, Seikan. *The Cave of Poison Grass.* Arlington, Va.: Great Ocean Publishers. Paperback.

Luk, Charles, trans. *Empty Cloud: The Autobiography of the Chinese Master Hsu Yun.* Rochester, N.Y.: Empty Cloud Press, 1974. Paperback.

Sasaki, Joshu. *Buddha is the Center of Gravity.* Translated by Fusako Akino. San Cristobal, N.M.: Lama Foundation, 1974. Paperback.

Shibayama, Zenkei. *A Flower Does Not Talk.* Translated by Sumiko Kudo. Tokyo: Charles E. Tuttle Co., 1970. Paperback.

WORKS OF SIGNIFICANT PAST MASTERS

Dōgen Kigen. *Shōbōgenzō: The Eye and Treasury of the True Law.* Translated by Kosen Nishiyama and John Stevens. Sendai, Japan: Daihokkaikaku Publishing Co., 1975. Volume 1.

Masunaga, Reiho. *A Primer of Soto Zen: A Translation of Dōgen's Shōbōgenzō Zuimonki.* Honolulu: University of Hawaii Press, 1971. Paperback and hardcover.

Reps, Paul, ed. *Zen Flesh, Zen Bones.* New York: Doubleday and Co., Anchor Books. Paperback.

Sasaki, Ruth Fuller, with Yoshitaka Iriya and Dana R. Fraser. *The Recorded Sayings of Layman Pang.* Tokyo and New York: John Weatherhill, 1971.

Snyder, Gary, trans., *Cold Mountain Poems: 24 Poems of Han Shan.* Portland, Ore.: Press-22, 1956. Paperback.

Stryk, Lucien, and Takashi Ikemoto, ed., and trans. *Zen: Poems, Prayers, Sermons, Anecdotes, Interviews.* New York: Doubleday and Co., Anchor Books, 1963. Paperback.

Suzuki, D.T. *Sengai, the Zen Master.* London: Faber and Faber, 1971.

Yampolsky, Philip B., trans. *The Zen Master Hakuin: Selected Writings.* New York: Columbia University Press, 1971.

INDEX

ABOUT THE CONTRIBUTORS

Kōryū Ōsaka Roshi: A lay Zen master in the Rinzai tradition, Kōryū Roshi is successor to Hannyakutsu Jōkō Roshi. His special contribution to Zen has been in his emphasis on the practice of lay persons. Kōryū Roshi is presently head of the Musashino Hannya Dojo, and president of Shakamunikai, an independent organization of Zen Buddhists in Japan.

Taizan Maezumi Roshi: A Soto Zen priest, Maezumi Roshi is successor to masters representing three major lines of Zen teaching: Hakujun Kuroda Roshi, Hakuun Yasutani Roshi, and Koryu Osaka Roshi. He is Director and resident Zen master of the Zen Center of Los Angeles, and Co-Editor of the Zen Writings series.

Bernard Tetsugen Glassman: A student of Maezumi Roshi's since 1968, Tetsugen is Senior Training Monk and Assistant Director of Zen Center of Los Angeles, and Co-Editor of the Zen Writings series.

John Daishin Buksbazen: A student of Maezumi Roshi's since 1969, Daishin serves as Pastoral Counselor and Vice President of Zen Center of Los Angeles, and is Publishing Editor of the Zen Writings series.

Dana Fraser: While a student of Kajitani Sōnin Roshi for six years at Shōkokuji Monastery in Japan, Dana collaborated with Ruth Fuller Sasaki and Prof. Yoshitaka Iriya, the leading Japanese specialist in colloquial Sung and T'ang Dynasty Chinese literature, in translating Buddhist texts. He has been translating with Maezumi Roshi since 1974.

Peter Kakuzen Gregory: Currently working on a Ph.D. in East Asian Languages at Harvard University, Kakuzen has studied with Maezumi Roshi since 1971. He has also studied under Koryu Roshi at the Hannya Dōjō in Japan, while there on a language-study fellowship.

Paul Turner: A freelance photographer living in Los Angeles, Paul has specialized in photographing people for the past eight years. An active backpacker, he spends as much time as possible hiking and photographing in the high Sierras.

The Zen Writings series is produced under the supervision of Series Editors Taizan Maezumi Roshi and Tetsugen Glassman Sensei. *Publishing Editor:* John Daishin Buksbazen. *Design consultants:* Sy Edelstein, Paul Turner. *Contributing artists:* Tom Andrews, Caribou, Mr. Endo, Emmett Ho, Manya Ekyo Maezumi, Gary Sotetsu Sekerak, Paul Turner. *Production Staff:* Tom Jishu Schulz, Lou Ryoshin Gross, Ed Kenzan Levin, Jocelyn Myoen Jacks, Adele Myoku Silvers, Brenda Chiko Beck, Susan Myoyu Palmer, Helen Glassman, Chris Ryogen Fang, Joan Jōan George, Sheldon Herman. *Distribution:* Paul Genki Kahn. *Typesetting:* Valtype, Los Angeles, California. *Printing and Binding:* Braun-Brumfield, Inc., Ann Arbor, Michigan.

The Paulownia leaves-and-flowers design is traditional in Japan, where in slightly different form, it serves as the crest of Sōjiji Monastery, one of two headquarters temples of the Soto School of Zen Buddhism. In the form shown here, it is the crest of Kōshinji Temple in Ōtawara, whose Abbot, the Venerable Hakujun Kuroda Roshi, was Maezumi Roshi's principal Soto teacher. In the United States, it represents Zen Center of Los Angeles, publishers of the Zen Writings series.